OSPREY
PUBLISHING

The SA 1921–45: Hitler's Stormtroopers

David Littlejohn · Illustrated by Ron Volstad

Series editor Martin Windrow

First published in Great Britain in 1990 by
Osprey Publishing, Elms Court, Chapel Way, Botley,
Oxford OX2 9LP, United Kingdom.
Email: info@ospreypublishing.com

Series Editor: MARTIN WINDROW

British Library Cataloguing in Publication Data
Littlejohn, David, *1924–*
    The Sturmabteilung: Hitler's stormtroopers
    1921–45.—(Men-at-arms series; 220).
    1. Germany. Nationalsozialistische Deutsche
    Arbeiter—Partei. Sturmabteilung, 1921–1945
    I. Title   II. Volstad, Ron   III. Series
    943.085

    ISBN 0-85045-944-3

Filmset in Great Britain
Printed in China through World Print Ltd.

FOR A CATALOGUE OF ALL BOOKS PUBLISHED BY
OSPREY MILITARY AND AVIATION PLEASE CONTACT:

The Marketing Manager, Osprey Direct UK,
PO Box 140, Wellingborough, Northants,
NN8 4ZA, United Kingdom.
Email: info@ospreydirect.co.uk

The Marketing Manager, Osprey Direct USA,
c/o Motorbooks International, PO Box 1, Osceola,
WI 54020-0001, USA.
Email: info@ospreydirectusa.com

VISIT OSPREY'S WEBSITE AT:

www.ospreypublishing.com

Acknowledgements

The author gratefully acknowledges the assistance of:
John R. Angolia, Klaus Benseler, Josef Charita,
Andrew Mollo, Karl Ortmann, Ulric of England,
Andrew S. Walker, Stewart Wilson.
    NB: The credit 'Walker Collection' refers to the
collection of the late Andrew Walker now in the
Imperial War Museum, London. Andrew S. Walker
(listed above) is no relation.

Artist's Note

Readers may care to note that the original paintings
from which the colour plates in this book were
prepared are available for private sale. All
reproduction copyright whatsoever is retained by the
publisher. All enquiries should be addressed to:

Ronald B. Volstad
P.O. Box 2730
Canmore, Alberta
Canada TOL OMO

The publishers regret that they can enter into no
correspondence upon this matter.

The SA 1921–45: Hitler's Stormtroopers

History of the Sturmabteilung Organisation

In 1919 Adolf Hitler joined the tiny German Workers' Party (DAP) in Munich, becoming its leader the following year and adding 'National Socialist' to its title. Thus the NSDAP, popularly known as the Nazi Party, was born.

All political parties had strong-arm squads to protect their meetings from disruption by rivals, and the NSDAP was no exception. In August 1921 ex-naval Lieutenant Hans Ulrich Klintzsch took command of the NSDAP's 'Defence and Propaganda Troop' which, the following month, was renamed the SA (*Sturmabteilung* = Storm Detachment). That November the SA had its 'baptism of fire' when the Communists attempted to break up a Nazi meeting in the Hofbräuhaus in Munich; although outnumbered, the SA gave their adversaries a bloody nose.

In 1922 the NSDAP created a youth section (*Jugendbund*) for males between the ages of 14 and 18 years. It was sub-divided into two age groups, the elder of which, for 16 to 18-year-olds and titled *Jungsturm Adolf Hitler*, was in effect a junior SA. Its successor, the Hitler Youth, remained under SA command until May 1932.

Originally confined to Munich, the SA made its first important sally outside that city when, on 14/15 October 1922, it took part in a 'German Day' at Coburg which resulted in a pitched battle with the Communists who held sway there. The 'Battle of Coburg' succeeded in breaking the hold of the Red Front in the city, and the press coverage which this incident achieved served to make Hitler's name known to a wider public.

The first 'national' rally of the NSDAP was held on 28 January 1923 when some 6,000 SA men

Capt. Röhm wearing first design *Stabschef* patches: twin gold oak leaves.

paraded before Hitler, who presented *Standarten* (standards) to four recently formed SA units: München, München II, Nürnberg and Landshut. A 'battle flag' (*Sturmfahne*) was, at the same time, conferred upon an SA company from Zwickau—the first SA unit to be formed outside Bavaria.

On 1 March 1923 SA Regiment Munich was formed. In the same month command of the SA passed to Hermann Goering after Klintzsch, a

Nuremberg, September 1923; the SA parade in the grey uniform of the period. (J. R. Angolia)

member of Captain Ehrhardt's *Freikorps*, was recalled by his chief following a quarrel between Ehrhardt and Hitler over their differing reactions to French occupation of the Ruhr. Goering brought with him the prestige of a hero of the First World War but was, by nature, indolent and self-indulgent. The true moving force behind the SA was Ernst Röhm, a staff officer at Army headquarters in Munich. It was Röhm who persuaded the military to supply the SA with arms, thus transforming it into one among several *Wehrverbände* (officially tolerated 'armed groups'—without exception anti-Communist).

In September 1923 Hitler succeeded in creating a *Kampfbund* (Fighting Union) of some 70,000 men, mainly SA but also *Bund Oberland* (a *Freikorps* unit) and *Reichs-Kriegsflagge* (an armed formation commanded by Röhm). On 9 November 1923 Hitler attempted to use this force to overthrow the Munich government. The badly planned, badly executed operation ended in humiliating defeat. The police opened fire on the demonstrators, killing 16 and wounding many more. Hitler was arrested; Goering, wounded, escaped to Austria. The SA was banned; those of its leaders who managed to avoid arrest fled to other German states where Bavarian law could not touch them. Hitler was given a five-year prison sentence but was released under an amnesty in December 1924. Röhm, protected by his army masters, received nothing worse than a 'severe reprimand'.

The failure of the *Putsch*, far from destroying the SA, served rather to spread it to other German regions. Refugees from Munich set up clandestine SA units under the name *Frontbann*. Hitler did not fail to draw the correct conclusions from this disaster. Armed insurrection against a government which commands the loyalty of the police and army is foredoomed. Henceforth he would employ only legal methods.

When the SA was re-activated in February 1925 Hitler categorically forbade it to bear arms or function as any form of private army. The days of the SA as a *Wehrverband* were over. Its purpose was to clear the streets of his political enemies. Hitler's view of the SA's rôle was hotly contested by Röhm, who envisaged it as a citizens' army, part of Germany's secret re-armament. The disagreement between the two became so bitter that Röhm resigned from the Party in April and in 1928 quit Germany for a military adviser's post in Bolivia.

The SA remained without an overall command (its various units each being accountable to their area *Gauleiter*) until November 1926, when Hitler named himself *Oberste SA Führer* (Supreme SA Leader). The actual executive leadership was vested in the Chief of Staff (*Chef des Stabes*). This post was entrusted to a prominent *Freikorps* leader, Franz Felix Pfeffer von Salomon[1] who set about organising the SA along military lines. It was now formed into:

Gruppen (the smallest unit)	*Standarten* (Regiments)
Trupps (roughly platoons)	*Brigaden* (Brigades)
Stürme (roughly companies)	*Gaustürme* (roughly Divisions)

A *Gausturm* corresponded exactly to an NSDAP *Gau*.

In August 1927 the SA numbered some 30,000 men. Two years later that strength had doubled. In 1930 a Motor SA was established to give greater mobility and allow a quick mustering of strength.

Despite his success in expanding the SA and increasing its efficiency, Pfeffer ceased to enjoy Hitler's confidence. It became apparent that Pfeffer's concept of the SA differed little from that of Röhm. Hitler discovered that Pfeffer had been secretly attempting to involve the Army in the para-military training of the SA. In August 1930 Hitler dismissed Pfeffer and telegraphed Röhm in Bolivia asking him to return and take charge of the SA. Röhm was back in Germany before Christmas and officially assumed duty as *Chef des Stabes* on 5 January 1931. He revised the structure of the SA, now dividing it into:

[1] Possibly because Salomon sounded Jewish, he preferred to be known as Franz Pfeffer or, incorrectly, Franz von Pfeffer.

Wilhelm Schepmann as an *Obergruppenführer*. (Josef Charita)

Scharen (the former *Gruppen*)	*Standarten*
Trupps	*Untergruppen* (the former *Gausturme*)
Stürme	*Gruppen*
Sturmbanne	

Under Pfeffer the highest SA formation, the *Gausturm*, had been subordinate to the Party leadership; but the new *Gruppe* had no NSDAP counterpart as it extended over several *Gaue*, and its leader (*Gruppenführer*) was thus answerable only to Röhm or, of course, to Hitler himself.

On 17/18 October 1931 a 'token mobilisation' of the Nazis' forces took place in the town of Brunswick, with around 104,000 uniformed participants. It was an impressive display of strength, but its very success alarmed the Weimar authorities. In December they imposed a ban on the wearing of *all* political uniforms. This proscription remained in force until the following June, by which time it had been demonstrated to have had little practical effect. The Nazis simply adopted a civilian 'uniform' of white shirt and black tie, and carried on as before.

In July 1932 Röhm created a yet larger SA agglomerate—the *Obergruppe* of which there were, at this stage, five. The SA now dominated the streets, disrupting the meetings of its rivals, and terrorising its opponents. Without actually challenging the government to a head-on confrontation, Hitler was able to blackmail and intimidate it with the size and discipline of his brown-shirted army.

On 30 January 1933, as a result of a combination of victory at the polls and back-stairs intrigues, Hitler was appointed Chancellor (Prime Minister) of Germany. The burning of the Reichstag building the following month was blamed on the Communists and used as the pretext for pushing through an enabling law which gave Hitler virtually dictatorial powers. Goering, Minister of the Interior for Prussia, authorised the SA to act as a police auxiliary and to sweep all 'enemies of the state' into concentration camps.

At the Party Day of Victory at Nuremberg that September, some 120,000 uniformed men participated.

Röhm was made a member of the Reichs cabinet as Minister without Portfolio. The number of SA *Obergruppen* had increased to ten by January 1934. But time was running out for the SA's most celebrated Chief of Staff. Röhm made no attempt to conceal his differences with Hitler over the rôle of the SA: an advocate of 'the second revolution', he wished to transform it into an armed force to supplement, even replace, the regular Army. Hitler, on the contrary, felt that the SA had already fulfilled its task of crushing its political opponents and now, with its rowdy behaviour, was becoming something of an embarrassment. He already looked ahead to a future war of conquest for which a fully professional army was essential. The Army, for its part, regarded the SA with undisguised contempt as 'brown scum', and was eager to co-operate with Hitler in expansion and re-armament.

Recklessly foolhardy, or naive to an incredible degree, Röhm continued publicly to voice his criticisms of his leader and to back them with scarcely veiled threats. Matters came to a head in the spring of 1934 when Hitler learned that Röhm was secretly arming his Staff Guards, something he had expressly forbidden. During June the SA was ordered to take a month's leave. On 30 June Hitler cut down its entire leadership in a single decisive blow. Dozens of SA men (and others) were shot dead by SS squads working from death lists prepared by Hitler and Goering. Röhm was arrested and, in prison, offered the chance to shoot himself. When he refused, he was shot through the window of his cell by his SS guard.

In Röhm's place Hitler appointed a loyal but colourless SA *Obergruppenführer*, Viktor Lutze, like all previous incumbents of the post a former Army officer. Lutze had to preside over the emasculation of the SA. On 20 July 1934 the SS, until this time subordinate to the SA Supreme Command, was granted its independence. The Motor SA was hived off and amalgamated with its 'junior partner' the NSKK to become a separate body. The *Flieger* SA was integrated into the German Air Sport

Photo *c.*1927 of SA and (in black képis) SS men. Note diversity of 'uniform'. (Ulric of England)

Viktor Lutze in Oslo, 1942, with officers of Quisling's *Rikshird* (Norwegian counterpart of the SA). Note black collar to greatcoat and long-service rings. (Josef Charita)

Organisation

Formation	Military Equivalent	Size
Schar	Squad	8–16 men
Trupp	Platoon	3–4 *Scharen*
Sturm	Company	3–4 *Trupps*
Sturmbann	Battalion	3–5 *Stürme*
Standarte	Regiment	3–5 *Sturmbanne*
Untergruppe/Brigade	Brigade	3–9 *Standarten*
Gruppe	Division	Several *Brigaden*
Obergruppe (1933–4)	Army Corps	Several *Gruppen*
OSAF	High Command	

Association, the SA *Feldjägerkorps* incorporated into the Prussian Police. The ten SA *Obergruppen* were abolished (although the rank *Obergruppenführer* was retained), the largest SA formation now being the *Gruppe*.

Despite these amputations and revisions, the numerical strength of the SA continued to grow. Thirty-six new *Standarten* were created in 1935, a further 25 in 1936, 30 in 1937 and 42 in 1938. Although membership was, as before, voluntary, there can be little doubt that many joined out of opportunism, since job prospects or advancement often depended on evidence of Nazi affiliation.

What now was to be the function of the SA? The leadership had no clear answer. The most favoured solution was that it should act as a sort of para-military sports club providing both physical and martial training although without, in the case of the latter, the actual use of arms. The SA might practise throwing grenades—but only wooden dummies! A secondary task was to assist in the dissemination of Nazi propaganda and to furnish—as it did dramatically each year at Nuremberg—a physical manifestation of the power and authority of the state. The rôle of the SA as a preparatory school for the armed forces was established only in January 1939 with the creation of the SA *Wehrmannschaften*.

In May 1943 Lutze was killed in a motor accident and was succeeded by Wilhelm Schepmann. When the *Volkssturm* was formed in October 1944 Schepmann was appointed its Director of Rifle Training, while Franz Pfeffer re-emerged from obscurity to take command of a *Volkssturm* brigade on the quiet Swiss border.

There were ten *Obergruppen* (Roman numerals I to X). After this configuration was abolished the highest formation was the *Gruppe*. In 1933 there were 21 SA *Gruppen* (plus one for Austria). By the outbreak of war this had risen to 25 and, with the incorporation of conquered territories, to 29.

At the OSAF (*Oberste SA Führung*) were Main Offices for Leadership, Personnel, Education, Health, Administration, *Wehrsport* and 'equestrian matters' (the semi-autonomous NSRI). Below the OSAF the *Gruppen* had corresponding staff departments and were responsible for running training schools (other than those at *Reichs* level).

Ranks (as from 1939)

Non-commissioned ranks	Military equivalent
SA *Sturmmann*	Private
SA *Obersturmmann*	Private 1st Class
SA *Rottenführer*	Lance Corporal
SA *Scharführer*	Corporal
SA *Oberscharführer*	Sergeant
SA *Truppführer*	Staff Sergeant
SA *Obertruppführer*	Sergeant-Major
SA *Haupttruppführer*	Regimental Sergeant-Major

Subalterns	
SA *Sturmführer*	2nd Lieutenant
SA *Obersturmführer*	1st Lieutenant
SA *Sturmhauptführer*	Captain

Middle ranking officers	
SA *Sturmbannführer*	Major
SA *Obersturmbann-*	Lt. Colonel
führer	
SA *Standartenführer*	Colonel

Senior officers	
SA *Oberführer*	No equivalent
SA *Brigadeführer*	Brigadier-General
SA *Gruppenführer*	Major-General
SA *Obergruppenführer*	Lt. General
SA *Stabschef*	Chief of Staff

Evolution of SA Uniform

At first Hitler's men were distinguished only by their *Kampfbinde*—a red brassard with a black swastika on a white circle—but gradually a species of uniform was evolved. By 1922 this consisted of a grey windjacket worn over a white shirt with grey breeches. Headgear was a dark blue or tan ski cap featuring some Nazi emblem or skull-and-crossbones (there was a wide diversity in this regard). A metal number, to indicate the unit, could be added to the centre of the swastika on the brassard, and a metal star below this to denote a squad leader.

By 1923 uniform had formalised into a field grey tunic worn closed at the neck but with white shirt and black tie just visible, and field grey breeches with either puttees or top boots. The tan-coloured ski cap had two buttons in the front below the black/white/red national cockade. Rank was indicated by white bands around the brassard:

Gruppenführer (Squad Leader): one band
Zugführer (Platoon Leader): two bands
Hundertschaftsführer (Company CO): three bands
Regimentsführer (Regimental CO): four bands

After the failure of the November 1923 *Putsch* the SA was banned, although it continued as the *Frontbann*, reverting to the windjacket form of dress and adding to the centre of the swastika (on brassard and flags) a black steel helmet.

When the SA was re-activated in February 1925 it went into brown shirts—a job lot of surplus German army tropical garb acquired in Austria the previous year at a bargain price! Breeches and képi

were likewise brown, albeit of various shades. Rank was, as previously, indicated by white bands around the brassard. In November 1926, when collar patches were introduced for the first time, the bands were replaced by one, two, three or four stars on the left collar to indicate rank. As the SA expanded, bars and oak leaves were added to accommodate new gradings.

A major change was the adoption in 1932 of a khaki tunic in response to a governmental demand that the SA 'should adopt a more respectable uniform'. In 1933 shoulder straps were introduced and coloured side panels added to the képi. In November 1933 the shade of khaki worn by the SA was darkened to 'olive-brown'.

Details of Uniform

Collar patches
In 1926 coloured collar patches were introduced: on the left was the rank insignia, on the right the unit numeral(s). *Standartenführer* and above wore rank on both collars. By contrasting the colour of the patch with that of the numeral(s) an attempt was made to reflect the *Landesfarben* (State colours) of the district—thus, units in Prussia had black patches with white numbers, those in the Hanseatic towns white patches with red numbers, etc. This arrangement proved difficult to sustain, and the colour combinations underwent a number of changes. The final arrangement is detailed below.

In August 1929 red collar patches were brought in for senior SA leaders.

Members of Staff of an *Obergruppe* had on the right patch the *Obergruppe* number in Roman numerals. Staff of a *Gruppe* had the *Gruppe* abbreviation (e.g. 'Sa' for Saxony) in Latin script. Staff of an *Untergruppe* had the abbreviation in Gothic script. Staff of a Brigade had 'Br' followed by the Brigade number (Arabic). Staff of a *Standarte* had the *Standarte* number (Arabic). Staff of a *Sturmbann* had the *Sturmbann* number (Roman) with an oblique stroke followed by the *Standarte* number (Arabic). Members of an SA *Sturm* had both *Sturm* and *Standarte* numbers in Arabic separated by an oblique stroke.

Collar patches for officers were piped in silver or gold bullion according to 'button colour'. Since there were not enough primary colours to go round, it was decreed in 1931 that two SA *Gruppen* would share the same colour and be distinguished by their buttons—silver or gold. During the period 1933–8 subalterns had patches piped in the twin colours of their *Gruppe*. Prior to 1939 collar patches of non-commissioned grades were unpiped, but thereafter *all* patches were piped in either yellow or white (according to their, by this time discontinued, 'button colour'—all buttons were now aluminium).

The symbols or letters worn on the collar patches of specialised SA formations (Medical, Motor, Signals, etc.) are detailed in the sections relating to these.

Collar piping
In July 1932 piping around the outer edge of the shirt/tunic/greatcoat collar was introduced. This was in the twin colours of the *Gruppe* for all ranks up to *Sturmhauptführer*. Higher ranks than this had gold

Goering in grey uniform with the unique brassard of SA Leader, September 1923.

Collar Patches (right side)
Row (a) Left to right): Staff of the Reichsführerschule; Staff of a Marine SA Training School; Staff of the National Sports School etc.
Row (b) Reserve Sturm of Standarte 20; Reserve Schar of Standarte 92; Flieger (Flying) SA Standarte 1
Row (c) Medical Sturm 6 of Standarte 2; Adjutant, 1929–1932; Sturm 22 of Gebirgs-Jäger Standarte 11
Row (d) Signals Training unit; Sturm 54 of the Leibstandarte; Sturm 13 of Standarte 16 (List)
Row (e) Pioneer Sturm of Standarte 13; Feldherrnhalle; Equestrian Sturm 6 of Standarte 62

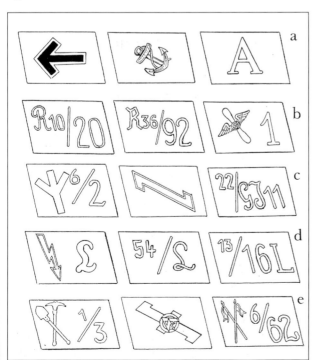

or silver piping according to button colour. In 1938 two-colour piping was abolished; all commissioned ranks had either gold or silver piping (as button colour).

The two colours listed under 'Piping' were those worn around the collar and/or collar patch as detailed previously.

Staff of *Gruppen*: bright red collar patches with silver piping. Subalterns (until 1938): bright red with red/white piping, thereafter silver.

Staff of the OSAF: carmine patches with silver piping. Subalterns (until 1938): carmine with carmine/white piping, thereafter silver.

Stabschef: bright red collar patches with gold piping.

The SA unit in the General Government (of Poland) wore grey collar patches piped in white with 'GG' on right side.

Personnel, up to the rank of *Oberführer*, on service outside Germany during the war wore brown

Summary of collar patches, piping, etc., as in May 1933

Gruppe	Abbr.	Collar patch	Number	Piping	Button colour	Rank 'bars'
Ostland	Ost.	dark wine red	w	black/white	g	silver/black
Westfalen	Wf.	dark wine red	w	black/white	s	silver/black
Niederrhein	Nrh.	black	w	black/white	g	silver/black
Berlin-Brandenburg	B	black	w	black/white	s	silver/black
Pommern	P	apple green	w	black/white	g	silver/black
Thüringen	Th.	apple green	w	red/white	s	silver/red
Westmark	WM	dark brown	w	black/white	s	silver/black
Niedersachsen	Ns.	dark brown	w	black/white	g	silver/black
Sachsen	Sa.	emerald green	w	white/green	s	silver/black
Nordmark	Nm.	emerald green	w	black/white	g	silver/black
Mitte	Mi.	orange yellow	b	black/white	g	silver/black
Südwest	SW	orange yellow	b	black/yellow	s	black/yellow
Schlesien	S	sulphur yellow	w	black/white	s	silver/black
Franken	Fr.	sulphur yellow	b	blue/white	g	black/blue
Hochland	Ho.	light blue	w	blue/white	s	silver/blue
Bayr. Ostmark	BO	light blue	w	blue/white	g	silver/blue
Oesterreich	Oe.	steel green	w	red/white	s	silver/red
Nordsee	No.	steel green	w	black/white	g	silver/black
Hansa	Ha.	navy blue	w	light blue/yellow	g	silver/light blue
Hessen	He.	navy blue	w	light blue/red	s	silver/light blue
Ostmark	Om.	pink	b	black/white	g	silver/black
Kurpfalz	KP	pink	w	black/white	s	silver/black

Notes

w = white   b = black   s = silver   g = gold

In the above, under Rank 'bars', the first mentioned colour is that of the bar, the second that of the central stripe. Thus silver/black = silver/black/silver. The names of the *Gruppen* are given in their German form: Sachsen = Saxony, Oesterreich = Austria, etc.

patches piped in white (silver for officers).

Members of *Hilfswerk Nordwest* (a unit of Austrian Nazi exiles in Germany) wore russet collar patches with 'NW' in white; the piping was red/white.

Shoulder Straps

Introduced in 1933 and, at this stage, worn on the right only, they were as follows:

(a) Non-commissioned grades: four strands in two colours (as per 'Piping') on an underlay in *Gruppe* colour.

(b) *Sturmführer* to *Sturmhauptführer*: four strands of silver or gold (as button colour) on underlay in *Gruppe* colour.

(c) *Sturmführer* to *Standartenführer*: three strands of intertwined silver or gold (abc) on underlay in *Gruppe* colour.

Summary of collar patches, piping, etc., as in 1940–5

Gruppe	Abbrev.	Collar patch	Piping
Tannenberg	T	dark wine red	yellow
Westfalen	Wf.	dark wine red	white
Niederrhein	Nrh.	black	yellow
Berlin-Brandenburg	B	black	white
Oder	O	pink	yellow
Südmark	Sm.	pink	white
Pommern	P	apple green	yellow
Thüringen	Th.	apple green	white
Mittelrhein	Mrh.	dark brown	yellow
Niedersachsen	Ns.	dark brown	white
Sachsen	Sa.	emerald green	white
Nordmark	Nm.	emerald green	yellow
Elbe	E	orange yellow	yellow
Neckar	N	orange yellow	white
Schlesien	S	sulphur yellow	white
Franken	Fr.	sulphur yellow	yellow
Hochland	Ho.	light blue	white
Bayernwald	BW	light blue	yellow
Nordsee	No.	steel green	yellow
Kurpfalz	Kp.	steel green	white
Hansa	Ha.	navy blue	yellow
Hessen	He.	navy blue	white
Donau	Do.	russet brown	yellow
Alpenland	Al.	russet brown	white
Sudeten	Su.	bluish grey	yellow
Weichsel	W	bluish grey	white
Warthe	Wa.	cornflower blue	white
Oberrhein	Orh.	cornflower blue	yellow
Böhmen-Mähren (Bohemia-Moravia)	——	unknown	——

By 1942 all collar patch numbers were white.

(d) *Oberführer* to *Obergruppenführer*: interwoven two strands of cord—one silver, one gold. Underlay: *Gruppe* colour.

(e) *Stabschef* (Röhm): as (d) but with six-pointed gold metal star. Underlay: bright red.

(f) *Stabschef* (1934–9): three interwoven gold strands. Gold metal oak leaf cluster. Underlay: bright red.

On 1 June 1939 underlay colour was changed for all ranks to the military concept of *Waffenfarbe* (a

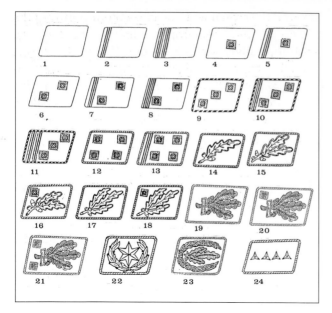

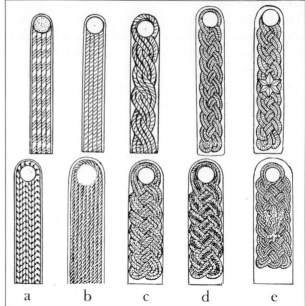

SA collar ranks. Worn on the left side only by ranks up to Standarten-führer, thereafter on both sides.
(1) SA Mann (after 1938: SA Sturmmann) (2) Sturmman (after 1938: (Obersturmman). (3) Rottenführer (4) Scharführer (5) Oberscharführer (6)Truppführer (7) Obertruppführer (8) Trupphauptführer (this rank, introduced in 1938, is sometimes called Haupttruppführer)

(9) Sturmführer
(10) Obersturmführer colour
(11) Sturmhauptführer
} Two colour piping discontinued in 1938, thereafter silver or gold as button colour

(12) Sturmbannführer (13) Obersturmbannführer (14) Standartenführer (15) Oberführer (16) Brigadeführer (17) Gruppenführer (18) Obergruppenführer

(19) Brigadeführer
(20) Gruppenführer
(21) Obergruppenführer
} Second design, 1944–45

(22) Stabschef (Röhm) (23) Stabschef (September 1934 to 1945) (24) Standartengeldverwalter: senior officer in SA Finance Department, 1931–1933

Shoulder straps
Upper row: 1932–1939 *Lower row:* period 1939–1945
abc = according to button colour (or former button colour)
(a) *Upper:* SA Mann to Obertruppführer: twin colours of SA *Gruppe* piping on an underlay is same colour as collar patch.
(a) *Lower:* brown with small silver Vs on Waffenfarbe underlay
(b) *Upper:* Sturmführer to Sturmhauptführer: silver or gold (abc) cord on underlay in collar patch colour
(b) *Lower:* "Silver" (matt aluminium) or gold (abc) on *Waffenfarbe* underlay.
(c) *Upper:* Sturmbannführer to Standartenführer: three strands of silver or gold (abc) interwoven cord on underlay in collar patch colour.
(c) *Lower:* As above but underlay in *Waffenfarbe*
(d) *Upper:* Oberführer to op Obergruppenführer: two strands (one silver, one gold) of interwoven cord on underlay in collar patch colour.
(d) *Lower:* Three strands (silver/gold/silver) on bright red underlay.
(e) *Upper:* Stabschef (Rohm) as above but with gold metal star, bright red underlay. After July 1934 the star was replaced by an oak leaf cluster.
(e) *Lower:* Stabschef (Lutze/Schepmann): gold cord, gold star, bright red underlay.

colour which indicated branch of the service) as follows:

Signals units	lemon
Equestrian units	orange
Pioneer units	black
Jäger/Schützen	green
Medical units	royal blue
Marine SA	navy blue
'Foot units'	grey
Gruppen staffs	bright red
OSAF staff	carmine

At this stage only the underlay was changed, the rest of the strap being unaltered except in the case of non-commissioned grades, who now had brown/white upon an underlay as above.

On the outbreak of war in September 1939 there was a change in the style of shoulder straps bringing them (for officer grades) more in line with military practice. They were now as follows:
(a) Brown flecked with silver Vs (two strands up, two strands down).
(b) Eight strands of silver or gold according to the former button colour ('button colour' was discontinued in 1938).
(c) Three interwoven strands in silver or gold.
(d) Three interwoven strands—two silver, one gold.
(e) Four interwoven gold strands and gold metal oak leaf cluster.

Headgear

The képi as introduced in 1925 had one (or two) silver button(s) on the front, otherwise no insignia. It was the same for all ranks until August 1929, when a red side panel (piped in silver) and silver piping around the crown was authorised for *Standartenführer* and above.

In 1929 a cap badge was created—an eagle holding a wreathed swastika; below it only one button was worn.

In 1931 piping in silver or gold 'according to button colour' (hereafter abbreviated to abc) around the flap and crown of the képi was authorised for *all* officers.

In March 1933 side panels in the *Gruppe* colour were added to all képis. Piping for commissioned grades was now revised to:
(i) Subalterns: two-colour piping in the *Gruppe* colours around the crown only.
(ii) Middle ranking officers: piping in silver or gold (abc) around the crown only.
(iii) Senior officers: silver or gold (abc) piping around the crown with the two-colour piping of the *Gruppe* around the upper edge of the flap. In addition, silver or gold (abc) *Tresse* braid was added to the upper edge of the flap below the two-colour piping. Width varied, 10, 15 or 20mm with ascending rank. After 1934 all such braid was silver except for (a) *Stabschef*: 20mm gold *Tresse*, bright red side panel; (b) Chiefs of Staff at *Gruppe* headquarters: 10mm wide gold *Tresse* interwoven with red thread, bright red side panel; (c) Section Heads (*Abteilungschefs*) at the OSAF: 10mm gold *Tresse*, carmine side panel.

In 1934 the cap badge was redesigned as a larger version of the preceding 'sharp-winged' eagle. In 1936 two new versions were tried out: one, with the eagle's head facing left, was quickly discontinued, the other was adopted for use by both SA and Political Leaders.

In 1938 two-colour piping was discontinued. All officer grades had silver or gold (abc); one year later

Wartime képi of *Stabschef* Lutze: bright red top with gold braid. (Adrian Forman)

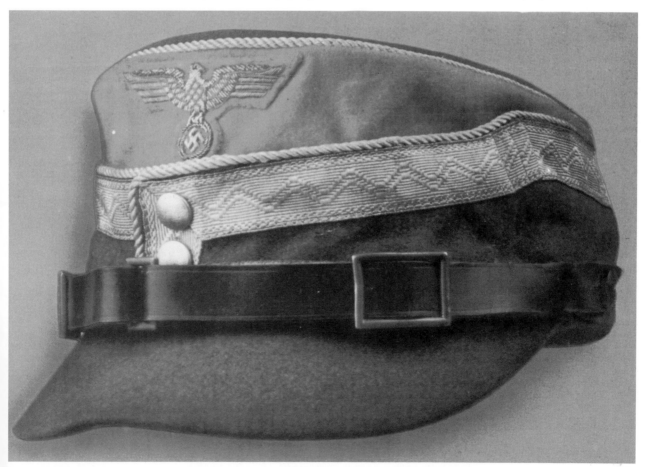

Képi of a subaltern of *Gruppe* Pomerania: light green side panel with black/white piping, gold button and silver 1929–34 type cap badge.

Belt Buckles

Before 1933 several unauthorised designs of buckles were produced and worn. Even after the institution of an official design—rectangular, with an eagle and wreathed swastika upon a circle whose lower half is oak leaves—minor variations were common.

In April 1934 a two-claw buckle was authorised for wearing with the tunic. A brocade belt with a round buckle for senior officers was created in 1938; it features the SA monogram on the chest of a closed-wing eagle with, at the base, an oak leaf wreath and, at the top, *Unser Führer, unser Glaube* ('Our Leader: our Faith').

Belt buckle; there are several variants, some with a 'mobile' swastika. (Karl Ortmann)

silver became standard—only the *Stabschef* had gold.

In addition to the képi the SA had a brown forage cap, the *Lagermütze* (camp cap), with a single silver or gold (abc) button on the front and, on the left side, a triangle in the *Gruppe* colour upon which was an eagle-and-swastika badge—normally woven, but also found in metal. The badge was, at first, of the 1929 design, later replaced by the 1936 type. Officers had gold or silver (abc) piping around the upper edge of the flap. In the Marine SA the *Lagermütze* was of the same design but in navy blue or white according to the order of dress.

The 'Italian' type of *Lagermütze* worn by the SA *Wehrmannschaften* is described hereafter.

In SA *Gruppe Hochland* (Highlands) an Edelweiss was worn on the side of the képi or *Lagermütze*, normally in metal but rarer cotton versions exist. At first this was the flower head only; later a swastika was added to the centre; finally a version with flower head, swastika and stock was created. This was usually worn on a cloth rhombus in the *Gruppe* colour.

Cap badges were always 'silver' (white metal or aluminium) and did not correspond to 'button colour'. Bullion versions for officers existed, but were rarer.

Cuff Titles

Certain SA *Standarten* were permitted to wear, on the lower left arm 15mm above the cuff, a 30mm-wide black band bearing the name of a fallen SA man. Over 50 such cuff titles exist, most to little-known individuals; only a few names, e.g. *Horst Wessel*, *Fritz Todt* and *Viktor Lutze* (awarded after his death to *Standarte* 99), are generally familiar. The type of lettering can be Gothic, semi-Gothic or *Sütterlin* (German hand-writing script)—the last being the rarer, possibly earlier, form.

In addition to personal names there were also a few commemorative titles of great distinction. Pre-eminent among these is *Stosstrupp Adolf Hitler*, awarded to veterans of the *Führer*'s original bodyguard. Almost equally illustrious were *SA-Regiment München 1923*, and *Der Kommandeur SA-Regiment München 1923*.

On a less lofty plane were those which merely indicated function or membership of a particular formation, e.g. *Ehrensturm* ('Honour Company'), *Leibstandarte* ('Bodyguard'—worn by SA Brigade 85 of *Gruppe Hochland*) or *Sturmbann z.b.V.* (*Sturmbann* 'for special duty') followed by, for example, *V/Wf* (No. 5 Westphalia). Members of the OSAF had a carmine cuff title with *Oberste SA-Führung*.

SA dagger with standard 'All for Germany' motto. (Andrew Mollo)

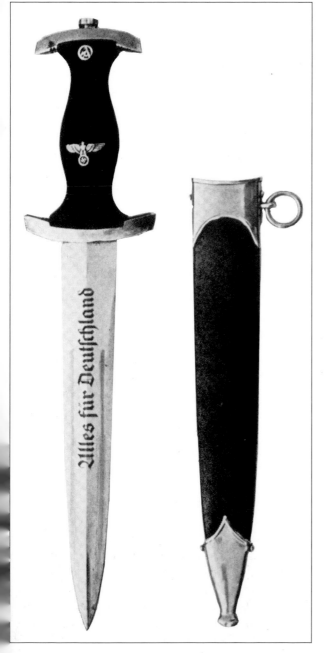

Adjutants' Insignia

At first SA adjutants wore a 'wolf-hook' (hooked bar) in silver bullion or metal on both collars—on carmine patches for adjutants to the *Stabschef*, on bright red for other OSAF adjutants. A gold wolf-hook was worn only by Hitler's adjutants.

In 1933 the customary way of indicating the rôle of adjutant—an aiguillette (looped ornamental cord worn from the right shoulder) replaced the wolf-hook collar device. Adjutants now wore normal rank insignia on the collar. Status was indicated by different coloured aiguillettes:

Gold silk: Hitler's adjutant
Gold cord: SA *Stabschef* adjutant
Silver cord: other OSAF adjutants
Scarlet/gold: *Gruppen* adjutants (1933–8)
Brown/silver: *Gruppen* adjutants (1939–45)

Adjutants on the Staff of a *Brigade*, *Standarte* or *Sturmbann* wore aiguillettes in the intertwined colours of their *Gruppe*, e.g. red/white for Thuringia and Austria; white/green for Saxony, etc.

Veteran Service Chevrons and Stripes

In February 1934 all SA personnel who had enlisted prior to 1 January 1933 were granted a gold chevron with two red stripes down the centre to be worn on the left upper arm; but in September of the same year this was discontinued and replaced by a scheme of rings worn around each cuff to indicate the actual year of joining. The rings, in silver-grey aluminium wire, were of two widths, 4mm and 12mm, and service was indicated thus:

Year	12mm ring	4mm ring
1925	2	2
1926	2	1
1927	2	—
1928	1	2
1929	1	1
1930	1	—
1931	—	2
1932 (to 30/1/33)	—	1

The above was unique to the SA; other uniformed formations continued to employ the chevron as the symbol of an 'old fighter'. The rings were worn round the cuff of all SA uniforms, including the greatcoat.

Daggers

The SA dagger, introduced on 15 December 1933,

SA *Sturmführer* with SA dagger with first type suspension, 1933. (J. R. Angolia)

long, was devised in 1937. This hangs from a double chain suspension of links alternately marked with a swastika and the SA monogram.

Daggers carried by the *Marine* SA had black wooden grips and sheaths (all others were brown), their metal parts being gilt (all others silver). In all versions, a metal SA monogram is inset at the top of the hilt and a metal eagle-and-swastika (two versions as per first and second design cap badges) inset in the middle of the hilt. Pommels and cross-guards were frequently individually numbered or lettered.

Privately presented daggers often had their blades inscribed with a suitable dedication. On the occasion of his 47th birthday (28 December 1937)

High Leaders dagger (1937) with double chain suspension. ('Old Brigade')

is sometimes referred to as the 'Holbein dagger' on account of its resemblance to a 16th-century Swiss dagger as shown in a painting by Hans Holbein. Its presentation, on completion of probationary service, indicated acceptance as a full SA member.

The blade was normally inscribed *Alles für Deutschland*, but those who had joined before 31 December 1931 received daggers inscribed *In herzlicher Freundschaft* ('In heart-felt friendship') *Ernst Röhm*. Some 125,960 daggers so inscribed were issued. After Röhm's murder all were either withdrawn or had their inscriptions erased.

A rather more ornate version for senior officers was created in 1935, with oak leaf ornamentation on the cross-guard and pommel, gilt (instead of silver) sheath and hilt fittings, and an oak leaf cluster above and below the wording on the blade. Its overall length is 37mm. A second version, 42mm

High Leaders dagger as worn by Lutze. (J. Charita)

Lutze was presented with a specially designed dagger by officers of the *Feldherrnhalle*. (Later, daggers of the same pattern were awarded to a number of high FHH leaders.) On his 50th birthday Lutze was given an honour version of its dagger by the Army, a unique feature of which was its elaborate hanger with the Wehrmacht eagle embroidered upon a scarlet cloth shield.

Flags and Banners

The Party flag was a black swastika in a white circle on a red field, thus combining the old Imperial colours. (The national colours under the Weimar Republic, as today, were black, red and gold.)

The first SA *Standarten* (banners) were presented to four SA Regiments on 28 January 1923. Somewhat reminiscent of the ancient Roman military banner, these took the form of a pole surmounted by a flying eagle holding a wreathed swastika, below which was mounted a rectangular 'box' with, on the front, 'NSDAP', and, on the reverse, a place name (in September 1933 this was reversed: place name on the front, 'NSDAP' on the rear). From this 'box' was suspended a red banner with a black swastika placed 'square' on a white circle and the motto *Deutschland Erwache* ('Germany

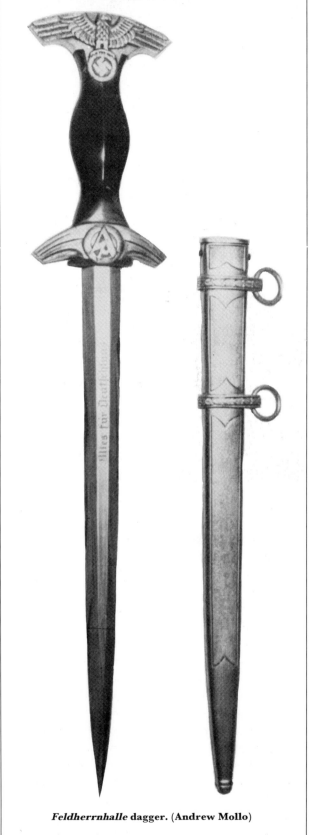

Feldherrnhalle **dagger. (Andrew Mollo)**

The flag of a recently formed *Standarte* is 'consecrated' by contact with the 'Blood Flag', 1931.

SA Standard-bearer's gorget.

the flag and bearing rank, forename and surname in Gothic lettering. If the fallen man had been a standard-bearer the ring was gold.

The banner of a Motor or Equestrian *Standarte* differed in that it hung from a wooden bar at right angles to the flag-pole and was without the NSDAP/place-name 'box'. Instead the unit designation appeared on the *Fahnenspiegel*.

Standard-bearers wore a metal gorget upon which was a 'star' with, in the centre, a facsimile of the centrepiece of the SA belt buckle (variants exist). The SA did not follow the military practice of having a standard-bearer's arm badge, although, pre-1933, unofficial arm badges were, on occasions, worn.

Command flags in the shape of rigid pennants on flag-poles were carried as unit 'markers' at large parades or, in slightly smaller versions, flown from the left-hand bumper of staff cars. These were square for a *Stabschef* (four consecutive designs) and senior leaders at the OSAF, *Gruppe* and *Standarte* level; triangular for *Untergruppe/Brigade* and *Sturmbann* commanders.

Awaken'); the inscription on the reverse was *Nat. Soz. Deutsche Arbeiterpartei Sturmabteilung*. The banner had a red/white/black fringe.

In Nazi usage *Standarte* meant both a banner and a regiment, thus when an SA unit achieved roughly regimental proportions it was awarded a banner which, in a pseudo-religious ceremony, was 'consecrated' by contact with the 'Blood Flag' — the flag carried during the abortive *Putsch* of November 1923 and stained with the blood of its fallen bearer.

A *Sturmfahne* (the flag of a *Sturm*) was red with a black swastika (often placed 'square') on a white circle. In the upper left corner was a *Fahnenspiegel*, a rectangle in the *Gruppe* colour with the unit numeral(s). This was originally outlined in the twin colours of the *Gruppe* (as per the collar piping) but later this was changed to silver or gold (abc).

A single *Sturmfahne* could be used for several *Stürme* (including Reserve ones), thus a number of such rectangles could appear (one above the other). In addition, the name of a fallen comrade could be woven into the fabric of the flag on a level with the *Fahnenspiegel* and to the right of it. Later this practice was dropped in favour of a streamer with the man's name attached to the flag-pole. Additional names of fallen comrades from the same unit could be added to the flag-pole in the form of silver rings, 15mm wide, attached below the level of

Special SA Formations

(1) Flieger (Flying) SA

In 1930 the SA established a flying branch; one year later the SS (still under SA command) did the same. As a sort of semi-civilian counterpart, the NSFK (National Socialist Flying Corps) was set up in 1932, but unlike the *Flieger* SA/SS, it was not regarded as a Party organisation.

Each SA *Gruppe* had its *Fliegerstaffel* (flying squadron) sub-divided into *Fliegerstürme* and *Fliegertrupps*. Each *Fliegersturm* embodied at least one *Lehrtrupp* (flying training flight).

Members of the *Flieger* SA wore standard SA uniform with a winged propeller on the right collar patch in silver or gold (abc). A combined SA/SS pilot's badge was devised incorporating the SA and SS monograms on silver 'wings' with an eagle-and-swastika in the centre. Later a more apposite (and less odd) badge replaced this. It features a silver wire circle with black dots (representing a propeller boss) with, in the centre, a black swastika, on either

Combined SA/SS pilot's badge. (Andrew Walker)

side silver bullion wings, the whole on a khaki background. The badge for other aircrew members is the same except that the central circle is red with white dots.

In September 1933 the *Flieger* SA was absorbed into the German Air Sport Association (DLV). Former *Flieger* SA/SS members could wear on the upper right arm of their DLV uniform a combined SA/SS monogram within a circle—both in silver bullion (gold for senior officers).

(2) Marine SA

In 1930 the SA formed *Marinestürme* (Naval companies), but it was not until 1934 that these became a separate entity.

Originally the *Marinestürme* wore the same colour of collar patch, shoulder strap, buttons, etc., as their parent *Gruppe*, but were distinguished by:

(a) Navy blue peaked cap in place of a képi.

(b) Navy blue, in place of brown, breeches.

(c) A fouled anchor in silver or gold (abc) on right collar patch.

With the creation of the *Marine* SA in 1934 all collar patches became navy blue, all rank insignia, buttons, etc., gilt. Shoulder straps for ratings were navy blue/white, those for officers gilt, the underlay for both being navy blue. In 1939 shoulder straps of *Marine* SA ratings were, as in the rest of the SA, brown flecked with silver Vs (on a navy blue underlay).

During the time that two-colour piping was worn around the collar and (for subalterns) also

Arm badge worn by former SA/SS men incorporated into DLV.

around the collar patch, this was royal blue/white. The gold metal anchor on the right patch was, after 1939, discontinued.

A single-breasted navy blue tunic was introduced in 1934 on which (as on other forms of dress) silver long-service rings might be worn—these should not be mistaken for rank insignia which, in the *Marine* SA, was exactly the same as in the rest of the service.

A white moleskin smock with trousers was worn as working dress by ratings. This was without collar patches, rank being indicated by a scheme of red 'bars', chevrons, and stars.

The working headgear for ratings was either the normal SA *Lagermütze* in navy blue (white for

summer) or the traditional German sailor's flat cap with a tally in cornflower blue on which appeared the unit designation in silver lettering (after 1938, gold lettering). In warm weather a white top could be worn with this or with the peaked cap.

'Swallows' nests' for *Marine* SA musicians were navy blue with gold 'bars'.

There were several variants of the cap badge. During 1930–7 it was the first design eagle-and-swastika in silver within a gilt oak leaf wreath—there are at least four variants of the wreath. After 1937 the gilt wreath (at least two variants) incorporated the SA monogram; above the wreath was the second design eagle-and-swastika in gilt metal.

There were several trade badges—a red cog-wheel for technicians, a red *blitz* for telegraphists (later changed to silver or gold according to level of skill), crossed red and white signal flags for signallers, etc. As in the German Navy, an Officer of the Watch clipped a gold metal badge, in the form of a fouled anchor within an oval wreath of oak leaves, to his left upper pocket while on duty.

The *Marine* SA was not restricted to Germany's sea coast; lakes and rivers often provided an opportunity to 'learn the ropes'. *Marine* SA units were also formed on board ocean-going German merchant vessels—the unit commander was not necessarily the ship's captain, or even one of its officers.

Staff, both commissioned and Petty Officers, at a *Marine* SA sports school wore a double-breasted

Marine SA with first design cap badge. (Ulric of England)

jacket in the style of a *Kriegsmarine* officer with, on the right cuff, the equivalent of the rating's cap tally, i.e. the place-name in white upon a cornflower blue band.

(3) Motor SA

Motortrupps and *Motorstürme* were created within the SA in April 1930, although it was not until the following year that the term *Motor* SA came into use. Just as the NSFK was envisaged as a non-Party back-up to the *Flieger* SA, so the NSKK (*Nat. Soz. Kraftfahrkorps*) was conceived as a civilian auxiliary to the *Motor* SA.

The following differences from normal SA uniform characterised the *Motor* SA:
(a) An M on the right collar patch.
(b) Black (or navy blue) breeches.
(c) A driver's badge on the left cuff.
This last, introduced in 1931, was a driving wheel

Marine SA officer's cap badge, final design. (Ulric of England)

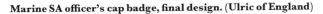

Members of an SA *Motorsturm* (possibly of *Gruppe Franconia*), early 1933. (Ulric of England)

upon which was an eagle-and-swastika, all on a black rhombus.

The placing of the M on the collar indicated whether the wearer belonged to:

(i) *Motorstandarte*: an M and single large numeral, worn by members of Staff.

(ii) *Motorsturm* within a non-motorised *Standarte*: an M and numeral in front of the oblique stroke.

(iii) *Motorsturm* within a *Motorstandarte*: an M after the oblique stroke (i.e. in front of the *Standarte* number).

On 23 August 1934 the *Motor* SA was amalgamated with the NSKK, which was now raised to the status of an independent party formation.

(4) Nachrichten (Signals) SA

The first Signals units of the SA were formed in 1930. Every *Standarte* was required to have one. Training included the use of signal lamps, morse code, wireless telegraphy, and messenger-dog handling.

At first members of Signals units wore, on the right collar patch, 'Na' (*Nachrichten*), but in 1933

this was replaced by a *blitz* (lightning flash) in the button colour. After the introduction of *Waffenfarbe* the *blitz* was discontinued and membership of a Signals unit was indicated by lemon yellow underlay to the shoulder straps.

As from 1935 holders of a Signaller's Certificate wore on the left cuff a red *blitz* on a brown oval, but in September 1939 the *blitz* was altered to silver or gold according to whether the man held one, or all three qualification certificates—(i) Wireless, (ii) Telegraphy, (iii) Messenger-dog handling. The German army and police still employed *Meldehunde* (messenger-dogs). Those of the SA had yellow dog-jackets with the SA monogram on either side.

A Signals Officer on the Staff of a *Gruppe* wore a *blitz* at a 45-degree angle on his right collar patch. Staff of the National Signals Training School had a white-outlined black *blitz* on a carmine right collar patch (also placed at a 45-degree angle).

(5) Pionier (Pioneer) SA

Among the several specialist units formed in 1930 was a Pioneer (or Engineer) branch. Its members were, initially, distinguished by 'Pi' (*Pionier*) on their right collar patches, but in 1933 this was replaced by a crossed pick and shovel in the button colour. With the introduction of *Waffenfarbe* this was discontinued and replaced by a black underlay to the shoulder straps.

Every *Standarte* had at least one *Pioniersturm*, and there were even entire *Pionierstandarte* (Pioneer Regiments).

Holders of a Pioneer's Certificate wore a silver pick and shovel device on a dark brown oval on the left cuff. In March 1939 a gold class was added.

An interesting, and unique, award to a Pioneer unit was the cuff title EMSLAND awarded to *Pionierstandarte* 10 of *Gruppe Nordsee* in recognition of its outstanding contribution to the land reclamation scheme in that region. Emsland (around the River Ems) is close to the border with Holland, and the German government copied the Dutch example and sponsored an enterprise to convert the marshes into farming land.

(6) Reiter (Equestrian) SA

The year 1930 also saw the setting up of equestrian units of the SA based on riding clubs, or in agricultural communities where riders provided their own mounts. After 1933 the *Reiter* SA was greatly expanded. It no longer relied on private horse ownership; every *Gruppe* was required to set up its own riding facilities.

Members of the *Reiter* SA wore, on the right collar patch, gold or silver (abc) crossed lances. Staff of the *Reitführerschule* (Equestrian Leaders School) in Berlin had gold crossed lances set at a 45-degree angle on a black collar patch. With the introduction of *Waffenfarbe* the lances badge was discontinued and replaced by a bright yellow underlay to the shoulder straps.

In March 1936 a National-Socialist Riding Corps (NSRL) was set up, theoretically separate from the *Reiter* SA; though its National Leader (*Reichsinspektor*) SA *Obergruppenführer* Litzmann was directly subordinate to the SA Chief of Staff. It may have been that the NSRL was intended to be for those who, for reasons of age or occupation, were ineligible for full SA membership. Certainly the NSRL remains a somewhat shadowy organisation with no (known) insignia of its own.

(7) Reserve SA

Although in semi-official existence for some two years previously, a Reserve SA was not formally set up until March 1929. It was for men over 40 years of age, or men precluded from full active membership by the nature of their employment. Reserve duties involved some three hours' attendance per week plus a fortnightly exercise.

Prior to 1933 the Reserve amounted to only around 20 per cent of the SA's total manpower, but after Hitler's accession its size and composition altered dramatically. In November 1933 it was divided into:

SA Reserve I (SAR I): men between 35 and 45 years.

SA Reserve II (SAR II): men over 45.

These two reserves absorbed the bulk of older members of the two principal war veterans' leagues—Steel Helmet and the *Kyffhäuserbund*. Members of these organisations under 35 were transferred to the active SA—a transfer in theory voluntary, but since refusal might be construed as unpatriotic, it was seldom resisted.

Following the 'Blood Purge' of June 1934 the structure of the Reserve was again changed. The SA was by now so vast and its services so little in demand that it was deemed expedient to remove even some of its younger element to the Reserve. The new structure comprised:

Active Reserve I: men between 18 and 35.

Active Reserve II: men between 35 and 45.

Inactive Reserve: men over 45.

In practice these age demarcations were not strictly adhered to, certainly not for officers.

When SAR I was formed its ex-Steel Helmet members continued to wear their former uniform with the addition of an SA képi, brassard and collar patches. On the right collar they had a metal 'R' and unit numeral. A chain-stitch 'R' appeared on the collar patch of all Active Reserve units. If placed before the *Sturm* number this indicated a *Reserve Sturm* of an active *Standarte*. If placed before the *Standarte* number, it indicated that the entire unit was Reserve.

During the existence of SAR II (November 1933 to August 1934) members wore the SA brassard with grey edges. Staff of the Departmental Chief of SAR II wore grey collar patches with, on the right, 'OL' (*Oberlandesführer*) in white.

In March 1937 there was a modification to the type of 'R' worn by Active Reserves I and II. Larger formations (*Stürme*, *Sturmbanne*, *Standarten*) had a Roman script 'R', smaller ones (*Scharen, Trupps*) an angular type of 'R').

Active Reserve I formations could be as large as Brigade strength (and had 'R.Br.' on the right collar). Active Reserve II were only up to *Standarte* level (with an 'R' before the *Standarte* number). In both cases the collar patch was in the *Gruppe* colour.

Inactive Reserve membership was indicated, not by an 'R', but by silver-grey collar patches, shoulder strap underlay and képi side panel.

(8) Sanitäts (Medical) SA

With violence frequently accompanying SA meetings, it was, from the very beginning, essential to have medically qualified persons on hand. Until 1932 such individuals were identified by either an arm band or, more usually, a 90mm circular cloth badge worn above, or in place of, the brassard. Doctors had a red cross on white; those with first-aid or ambulance experience had a white cross on red.

In October 1932 violet coloured collar patches were introduced for medically qualified personnel. Doctors with the rank of *Standartenführer* and above wore an Aesculapius staff (a snake around a stick) on both collars; officers below this rank on the right collar only. The same applied to pharmacists except that their emblem was an 'A' (*Apotheker*).

When coloured panels were added to the képi the medical colour was, as above, violet, as was the underlay to medical shoulder straps. Late in 1933 collar patch emblems were discontinued. In their place badges were worn on the left lower arm with the following symbols:
(a) Doctors: an Aesculapius staff.
(b) Pharmacists: a Gothic 'A' (in some cases Latin 'A').
(c) Dentists: a Gothic 'Z' (*Zahnarzt*).
(d) Veterinary surgeons: a snake (without the staff).
All the above were gold wire (more rarely, gilt metal) upon a violet oval piped in gold. Medical orderlies wore, as before, a white cross on a red circle on the upper left arm.

In 1934 there was a further change—a reversion to collar patch emblems, but this time placed behind both collar patches (which were now in the *Gruppe* colour). The symbolism was as above except that the 'A' and the 'Z' were Latin script. The colour of the emblems corresponded to the button colour and they were normally metal, less frequently bullion. Semi-qualified doctors and dentists (students in their final year) wore on the left cuff a 40mm brown circle with, in white cotton, respectively an Aesculapius staff and a Gothic 'Z'.

In November 1937 there was yet another alteration. The Nazis had by now decided that their medical symbol should henceforth be the so-called 'life rune'. Medical speciality was, as before, indicated by a badge worn on the lower left arm. Since all medical personnel had the 'life rune', their particular skill was indicated by the shape of the background as follows:
(a) Doctors: oval.
(b) Dentists: rectangular.
(c) Veterinary surgeons: a triangle pointing downwards.
(d) Pharmacists: a triangle pointing upwards.
All the above were in silver bullion on brown. Medical orderlies had a red 'life rune' on a khaki oval, also a metal 'life rune' in the button colour on the right collar patch. On the march, orderlies wore a white brassard with a red 'life rune', doctors the same but with red edges top and bottom.

With the introduction of *Waffenfarbe*, the underlay of medical branch shoulder straps became royal blue.

Staff and students at the National Medical School at Tübingen wore, on both collars, a carmine patch with a white-outlined black 'life rune'; officers had this patch piped in gold.

Other Specialist Sections

(1) Musikeinheiten (Music Units)

Every *Standarte* had its marching band (*Musikzug*), every *Sturmbann* its fife-and-drum corps (*Spielmannzug*).

Following long-established practice, bandsmen wore a form of shoulder ornamentation known as 'swallows' nests' (*Schwalbennester*). These were in the colour of the *Gruppe* with silver or gold (abc) vertical braid 'bars'. Ostland was an exception, with black 'bars' on a pink background. Initially all members of a *Musikzug* had a short fringe at the end of their swallows' nests, but this was altered in 1933

1: Leader, 1921
2: Zugführer, 1923
3: Truppführer, Gruppe Franken, Nov. 1926

A

1: Gruppenführer, 1928
2: Scharführer, Untergruppe Hamburg, 1932
3: Oberscharführer, Gruppe Nordmark, 1933

B

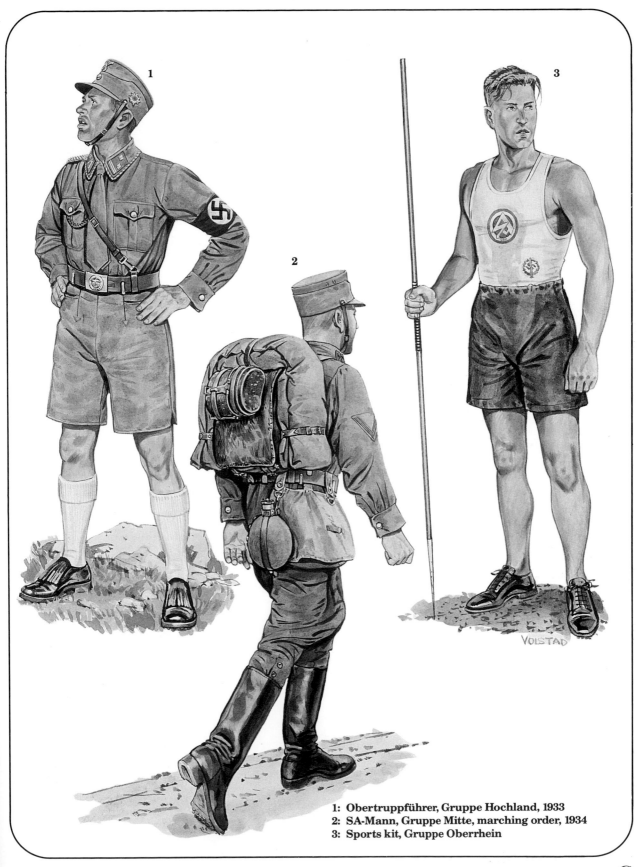

1: Obertruppführer, Gruppe Hochland, 1933
2: SA-Mann, Gruppe Mitte, marching order, 1934
3: Sports kit, Gruppe Oberrhein

C

1: Obersturmführer, Feldpolizei, Gr. Berlin-Brandenburg
2: Feldjäger-Rottenführer, 1934
3: Sturmann, Feldherrnhalle, 1939

D

1: Obersturmführer, Marine SA, 1934
2: Sturmbannführer, Marine SA Sea Sport School, 1934
3: Rottenführer, Marine SA white uniform

E

1: Sturmführer, Motor SA, Gr. Franken, 1933
2: SA-Spielmann, Gr. Hansa, 1934
3: Standartenführer (medical), Gr. Westmark,
   evening dress

VOLSTAD

F

1: Obergruppenführer, SA Gruppe Staff, 1939
2: Obersturmbannführer, OSAF, summer uniform
3: Haupttruppführer, Gr. Südmark, 1940

G

1: **Hauptsturmführer, Wehrmannschaft, Gr. Nordsee, 1942**
2: **SA-Mann, Wehrmannschaft, Gr. Niederrhein, 1944**
3: **SA-Mann, Wehrmannschaft, Styria, 1945**

and thereafter only the drum major of a *Musikzug* or *Spielmannzug* had a fringe (rather longer than before—about 7mm). The bandmaster, or conductor (*Musikzugführer*) did not wear swallows' nests, nor did any officer whose function was that of director of music. Swallows' nests were detachable, being clipped to the end of the shoulder by metal hooks and were worn only during 'music-making.

In addition to their swallows' nests, SA musicians were, in 1931, granted a collar device—a Greek lyre. Between 1931 and 1933 musicians' collar patches were piped in the twin colours of their *Gruppe* (a practice normally restricted to subalterns). No rank insignia were worn by non-commissioned grades during this period; in its place a large metal lyre (in the button colour) was displayed on the left collar and the unit number on the right. The *Musikzugführer* wore the three stars of a *Sturmführer* (and also a small lyre). After 1933 musicians wore the lyre on the right with standard rank insignia on the left.

No size for a *Musikzug* was laid down; a *Spielmannzug* usually comprised about 24 men.

(2) Jäger and Schützen Units

Jäger

The word *Jäger* in German means both a huntsman and a light infantryman. It is appropriate that this should be so, since the light infantry component of the German and Austrian armies was traditionally drawn from professional huntsmen and foresters. The SA sought to maintain the *Jäger* tradition in those parts of Germany and Austria from which the former *Jäger-Regimenten* had been drawn. The traditional *Jäger* green was used for the 'J' which appeared on the right collar patch, its shade contrasting with the *Gruppe* colour of the patch— light green on dark patches, dark green on light ones.

In May 1915 Mountain Light Infantry Regiments (*Gebirgsjäger-Regimenten*) had been created as part of the German Alpine Corps. This tradition, too, was carried over by the SA for units raised in the mountainous regions of southern Germany and Austria. Their right collar patch had a green 'GJ' (as above in contrasting shades). Some SA *Gebirgsjäger-Standarten* in Austria wore for a time an Edelweiss (head and stock) on their right collar patch before this was replaced by the 'GJ' patch.

SA bandsmen, *c.*1931

Schützen

A Rifle (or Sharpshooters) Battalion (*Schützen-Bataillon*) sometimes formed the third battalion of a German infantry regiment, often functioning in a semi-independent capacity. Again, this tradition was adopted by the SA. On their right collar patch SA *Schützen-Standarten* had an 'S' in a shade of green, as before contrasting with the *Gruppe* colour. The SA also raised *Gebirgsschützen-Standarten* (Mountain Rifle Regiments) in an attempt to combine the skills of alpinism and marksmanship. These units had 'GS' on the right collar—again in a shade of green which contrasted with the *Gruppe* colour.

With the introduction of *Waffenfarbe* the shoulder strap underlay for all the above was changed to green and, a little later, the green lettering on the collar patch was altered to white. These 'mountain' formations of the SA had the right to wear an Edelweiss on the left side of their caps.

Ski-ing instruction formed part of the mountain training, and the SA had its own 'mountain tunic' (*Bergrock*) for this and rock-climbing. It was generally similar to the normal tunic except that

33

Badge worn on left upper arm, in place of brassard, by senior SA leaders during the war: gold wire on carmine backing. (J. R. Angolia)

the lower pockets were concealed (only the flaps showing) and the cuffs were elasticated to fit closely to the wrist, allowing gloves to be worn over them. The trousers worn with the *Bergrock* were tapered and close-fitting at the ankles, where they laced up so that heavy climbing boots could be secured over them.

Originally some *Jäger* collar patches featured a hunting horn, but this practice was forbidden by an order of August 1934 which stated that the use of a *Jagdhorn* as a collar device was 'unauthorised' and that it had to be replaced by a 'J'.

As in the rest of the SA, no unit was actually armed. For training purposes small-bore rifles (usually from existing gun clubs) were borrowed.

(3) Leibstandarte

In Munich an SA unit known as the *Leibstandarte* (Bodyguard) was stationed. It was not for Hitler's personal protection (that was the exclusive prerogative of the SS), but a ceremonial formation possibly intended to carry the tradition of the former Royal Bavarian Bodyguard Regiment once quartered in that city. On their right collar, members wore a script 'L' on the light blue patch of *Gruppe Hochland*.

(4) Standarte List

During the First World War Hitler served in the 16th (Reserve) Infantry Regiment. Following

German custom, the regiment was better known by the name of its commander, thus it was popularly referred to as Infantry Regiment List. Although a Bavarian regiment, its 'tradition' was awarded to *Standarte* 16 of *Gruppe Berlin-Brandenburg*. Members of this unit wore a block type 'L' in white on the black collar patch of their *Gruppe*.

(5) Finance Department, 1931–3

No one in the SA, apart from a few senior officers, was paid, but that is not to say that the SA was unconcerned with financial matters. A Financial Administrative Branch (*Geldverwaltung*) was established in 1931 with special collar devices for its members. Ranks were:

(i) *Gruppengeldverwalter*: a silver laurel leaf on a red patch on both collars, piped in silver.

(ii) *Untergruppengeldverwalter*: silver or gilt (abc) laurel leaf on left, *Untergruppe* abbreviation on right collar, piped in gold or silver (abc).

(iii) *Standartengeldverwalter*: four silver three-pointed stars on left side, on right *Standarte* numeral. Collar patches in *Gruppe* colour, piped in silver.

(iv) *Sturmbanngeldverwalter*: three silver three-pointed stars on left collar, on right *Sturmbann/Standarte* numerals. Collar patches in *Gruppe* colour, piped in twin colours of *Gruppe*.

(v) *Sturmgeldverwalter*: two silver three-pointed stars on left, on right *Sturm/Standarte* numerals. Unpiped patches in *Gruppe* colour.

(6) Administrative Officials

In May 1933 the above collar devices were

Instructors at the SA Sport School at Hamm wearing the special *Übungsanzug* uniform. (J. R. Angolia)

discontinued and the Finance Department was absorbed into a broader general Administrative Branch. New ranks such as *Oberverwaltungsführer* and *Stabsrechnungsführer* were dreamt up, but quickly jettisoned in favour of the more logical use of existing SA ranks prefixed by *Verwaltungs* (Administrative), thus an SA *Obertruppführer* in this branch became an SA *Verwaltungsobertruppführer*.

Commissioned grades wore silver shoulder straps on a light blue underlay, non-commissioned ranks four parallel strands of light blue cord on a light blue underlay. All collar patches were light blue with silver insignia. The képi side panel was likewise light blue.

In March 1934 there was a major revision. All collar patches, insignia, képi side panels, etc., reverted to normal SA practice of *Gruppe* colour—administrative function was now indicated by a metal 'V' (occasionally bullion) worn behind the collar patch on both sides. In 1937 the 'V' was dropped and the Administrative Branch had light blue piping around all collar patches (in the case of officers, the blue was the inner colour, gold or silver the outer piping). In October 1941 the use of blue piping was discontinued.

(7) RZM (Reichszeugmeisterei)

In 1929 the SA set up a Quartermaster's Department to regulate uniform and provide it as economically as possible. After Hitler's accession to power a National Quartermaster's Department (*Reichszeugmeisterei*) was established which had legal powers to control all NSDAP uniforms and their costs. Only firms granted an RZM contract could supply Party insignia, thus ending the flow of unofficial or semi-official pieces. All official items were now RZM marked or labelled.

RZM personnel had special collar ranks described (in an order of October 1932) thus:

(i) *Reichszeugmeister*: a 'golden scalloped leaf' (*goldenes gezachtes Blatt*) on both collar patches, piped in gold.

(ii) *Vorstände der Zeugmeistereien* (Directors of QMe depôts): a golden scalloped leaf on left patch, golden 'ZM' on right, piping gold.

(iii) *Angestellte der Zeugmeistereien* (employees at QM depôts): normal SA ranks on left, gold 'ZM' on right.

The following year the 'golden scalloped leaf' was replaced by the oak leaf of a *Standartenführer*. In 1929 the collar patch colour was blue, but in 1933 this was changed to carmine.

(8) Eisenbahneinheiten (Railway Units)

Railway units of the SA existed briefly in Austria. Their right collar patch featured a winged railway wheel. One unit had an 'E' (*Eisenbahn*) interwoven with the number '1' on its right collar commemorating the shoulder insignia of a former prominent Austrian railway formation.

(9) Reichsautozug Deutschland (RAZ)

Hitler was so impressed by the work of SA *Sturmführer* Schäffer with his loudspeaker vans during the election campaign of 1933 that he placed him in charge of a special mobile propaganda unit known as *Reichsautozug Deutschland* (National Motor Squad Germany). Members of this small formation had, as their working uniform, a brown boiler suit with two breast pockets, worn open-necked with a khaki shirt and black tie. The normal SA brassard was worn with, below this on the cuff, a black band with *Reichsautozug Deutschland* in white. Headgear was a brown beret piped in black. Dress uniform was standard SA with red collar patches and shoulder strap underlay. On the right collar 'RAZ' was displayed in white, on the left normal rank insignia. Both patches piped in white.

In 1937 the RAZ was disbanded.

'Police' and Para-Military SA Formations

(1) Stabswachen

One of the tasks of the SA had always been the protection of Party meetings and speakers, but it was not until 1933 that regular security units, known as *Stabswachen* (Staff Guards) were formed. In these, service was full-time with a minimum enlistment of 12 months. Members wore normal SA

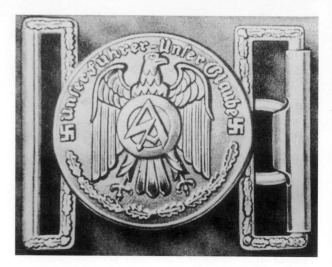

Senior Leaders belt buckle with motto 'Our Leader, our faith'. (J. R. Angolia)

uniform with one of the following cuff bands on the lower left arm:
Stabschef: gold Sütterlin script on carmine with gold edges (Röhm's personal bodyguard).
Stabswache: white Sütterlin script on bright red for guards at *Gruppe* and *Obergruppe* headquarters.
Stabswache: Gothic script in colour of collar patch lettering on band in colour of collar patch for guards at any headquarters below *Gruppe* level.

The above existed between February 1933 and March 1934; thereafter and until the elimination of Röhm in June '34, the following were used:
Stabschef Röhm: gold Gothic script on carmine band with gold edging.
Adolf Hitler: grey Gothic script on black with grey edges for members of SA *Standarte* 'Adolf Hitler'.
Stabswache Göring: silver Gothic script on bright red band with silver edging.
Stabswache: Gothic script in colour of collar patch lettering (with edging in same colour) on a band in colour of collar patch, e.g. black lettering on a yellow band with black edges: Headquarters guard of SA Group Franconia.

The right collar patch for OSAF staff guards was plain carmine; that for *Stabswache Göring*, plain red; others in *Gruppe* colour with *Gruppe* abbreviation.

On duty a steel helmet could be worn.

(2) Streifendienst

The SA had its own police or 'patrol' service, the *Streifendienst*, under the control of a local area commander (*Standortführer*). On duty members wore, at first, a 110mm-wide yellow brassard with, in black, *Standortführer Streifendienst*; later a 60mm-wide black cuff band with, in white or grey Gothic lettering, *Der Standortführer*, below this a place name, e.g. *Blankenburg a. H.* (am Havel). Half-width (30mm) versions also exist, e.g. *Standortführer-Grunstadt* (grey on black, no edging), and *Der Standortführer Stockach* (grey on black with grey edges).

(3) Hilfspolizei/Feldpolizei of Berlin-Brandenburg

After Hitler attained power in January 1933 he appointed Goering Minister of the Interior of Prussia. Since Prussia controlled some two-thirds of Germany, it was a post of considerable power. Goering ordered the police to act ruthlessly against 'all enemies of the state'. To assist them in this task he created, in February 1933, a Police Auxiliary (*Hilfspolizei*) from among the SA/SS. At first they wore only their existing uniform with a HILFSPOLIZEI brassard (various designs), but the following month, now renamed Field Police of the Berlin-Brandenburg Group (*Feldpolizei der Gruppe Berlin-Brandenburg*), their SA/SS uniform was modified in the following manner:

(a) On right collar patch a silver Prussian police star.

(b) A similar star in place of button on képi.

(c) A blue police greatcoat in place of brown SA one.

(d) A police gorget (worn on duty).

Collar patches were black, piped in black/white. The gorget was silver with the Prussian police star in the centre and a swastika in either corner. When the gorget included the unit number (not all did) this appeared below the police star.

(4) Feldjägerkorps (FJK)

In October 1933 the *Feldpolizei* was renamed the *SA Feldjägerkorps* (roughly: Military Police) and given a distinctive olive-brown uniform, comprising a police-style tunic, breeches and brown top boots. Belt and cross-strap were brown leather, the buckle being of the SA variety—gilt with a silver centrepiece. The greatcoat was olive-brown but with a dark brown collar (senior ranks had also dark brown revers). Headgear was an SA képi in the same colour as the tunic with a white side panel

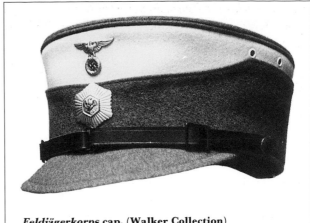

Feldjägerkorps cap. (Walker Collection)

and, on the front, a gold police star beneath a silver eagle-and-swastika. Collar patches were white with, on the right, a gold police star, and were piped in gold for senior officers, in black-and-white for subalterns, unpiped for others. Rank, on the left patch, was standard SA with gold stars and silver 'bars'. The *Führer des Feldjägerkorps* had a 15mm gold *Tresse* around the turn-up of his képi.

All ranks wore a white lanyard and, when on duty, a gorget similar to that of the *Feldpolizei* which normally featured an 'A' (*Abteilung*) followed by a Roman numeral 'I' to 'VI b' for one of the eight *Abteilungen* (main units). Below the centrepiece star an Arabic numeral denoted the *Bereitschaft* (or sub-unit of around 60 men).

Headquarters was *Abteilung* III b in Berlin. A white cuff title with *III B Berlin* in gold exists (there may have been others). All FJK personnel wore the standard SA brassard. The sports singlet emblem was a police star with two swastikas above it and 'FJK' (Gothic script) below.

As 'police' the FJK were allowed to carry revolvers and a dress bayonet, officers a ceremonial sword. On duty a steel helmet was worn.

Goering latterly lost interest and, on 1 April 1935, handed the FJK over to the Prussian *Schutzpolizei*. Thereafter it ceased to have any connection with the SA.

(5) Standarte 'Feldherrnhalle'

After the death of Röhm the various *Stabswachen* were disbanded and replaced by a single *SA Wachstandarte* (Guard Regiment). At first conceived simply as a ceremonial formation, it was, after March 1935 and the re-introduction of compulsory military service, envisaged as an élite regular body which would provide para-military training for the rest of the SA. Any man who had belonged to the SA for at least six months was allowed, if he so wished, to do his two-year conscript service in this unit. In September 1936 the name was changed to *SA Standarte 'Feldherrnhalle'* (from the historic building in Munich which embodied a shrine to fallen Nazis of November 1923).

On 12 January 1937, to celebrate Goering's 44th birthday, Lutze nominated him 'Honorary Commander-in-Chief of the *SA Standarte "Feldherrnhalle"*'. The SA's *Stabschef* had intended this to be no more than a symbolic gesture, and was more than a little taken aback when Goering incorporated the entire *Standarte* into his newly formed *Luftwaffe!*

For the following two years the *Feldherrnhalle* operated under a dual command—SA and *Luftwaffe*—a fact reflected by its uniform: for 'walking out', SA brown with the *Luftwaffe* eagle above the left breast pocket; for service dress, standard *Luftwaffe* blue-grey, in both cases with SA collar ranks on the left. The right collar had at first a white Gothic 'W' (*Wach*) on carmine, but in 1938 this was replaced by a 'wolf hook' with the SA monogram in the centre.

Lutze's vision of the *Feldherrnhalle* as a training formation for the SA was never realised. It did not function as a single entity but as seven separate *Sturmbanne* in different German cities. With the coming of war the bulk of the *Feldherrnhalle* was incorporated into the armed forces—into the

Duty gorget for *Feldherrnhalle*.

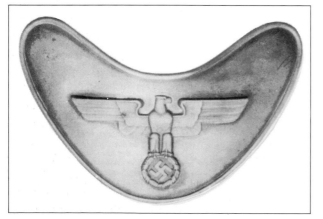

Luftwaffe as an Air-Landing Battalion (later a Parachute Regiment), into the army as a battalion of Infantry Regiment 271. In August 1942 *Grenadier* (the new term for Infantry) *Regiment* 271 was granted the title '*Feldherrnhalle*'. In June 1943 it was raised to divisional strength as *Panzergrenadier-Division Feldherrnhalle*. Badly mauled in the fighting on the Eastern Front, it was disbanded in July 1944.

A cuff title *Feldherrnhalle* in silver Sütterlin script on brown was worn by units in the Reich and, after September 1942, by *Grenadier Regiment* 271 and its successor. In July 1943 all *Feldherrnhalle* formations, home-based or Army, were granted the right to wear on both shoulder straps the SA monogram on three horizontal *Kampfrune* crossed by one vertical one—in bronze for men and junior NCOs, silver for senior NCOs, and gilt for officers.

The képi side panels for the *Wachstandarte* and *Feldherrnhalle* were carmine. Until 1939 shoulder straps for non-commissioned ranks were carmine/white on an underlay (for all ranks) of white. With the introduction of *Waffenfarbe* the underlay for home-based units was changed to grey; that for Army units was white (while infantry) and grass green on becoming *Panzergrenadier*.

A special gorget was worn when on duty, but a standard-bearer wore the normal SA gorget.

(6) SA Wehrmannschaften

By a decree of 19 January 1939 a new branch of the SA, the *Wehrmannschaften* (roughly: 'Militiamen'), was established, 'to undertake the pre- and post-military training of all German males'. It was to be responsible for the para-military education of the older age groups of the Hitler Youth and the reservist training of conscripts once they had completed their military service.

SA duty was voluntary, military service was not; thus every male would, eventually, find himself part of a Nazi-controlled organisation. War disrupted this grand design. There were no post-military-service conscripts—those called to the colours remained 'for the duration', and the pre-military training of the Hitler Youth was increasingly taken over by the SS. Also, of course, much of the regular cadre of the *Wehrmannschaften* was absorbed into the forces. In consequence the *Wehrmannschaften* functioned mainly as a back-up to the regular forces, for which purpose it was sub-divided into Army, Navy and Air Force sections, or as a general 'home front' auxiliary assigned to civil defence, police or any other body as dictated by the exigencies of war.

Only in northern Yugoslavia did it assume full combat status. After the fall of that country in April 1941 Lower Styria, Carinthia and Upper Carniola were incorporated into the Reich, and considerable partisan unrest followed. In 1942 obligatory military service in that region raised a *Wehrmannschaftsbataillon Süd* which was later expanded from one to five battalions to become *Wehrmannschaftsregiment Untersteiermark* (Militia Regiment Lower Styria). It participated in several major drives against the local partisans.

The *Wehrmannschaften* uniform was olive-brown, and comprised a tunic which could be worn open or closed at the neck, breeches with top boots for officers (trousers and army boots for others). An unusual feature was the 'Italian' forage cap—a unique example of a German borrowing from its Axis partner. This had, on the front, the SA cockade monogram and, on the left side, an eagle-and-swastika on a triangle, correctly black although *Gruppe* colour was sometimes used.

Rank was standard SA worn on collar patches in the *Gruppe* colour and piped in yellow or white according to the (former) button colour. Officers' shoulder straps were normal SA, but non-commissioned grades had round-ended straps in the same cloth as the tunic and piped in white for units serving with the Army, in navy blue for those

Model 43 service cap as worn by *Wehrmannschaft* units in Styria—see Plate H3. (Ulric of England)

with the *Kriegsmarine*, and yellow for those with the *Luftwaffe*.

The 'Italian' forage cap was often replaced by the M1943 field cap. An Edelweiss cap emblem was worn by units in the 'highland' *Gruppen*.

All ranks wore the normal SA brassard except the Styrian SA units, which had a brassard featuring the flame-breathing Styrian griffin on equal white and green (the Styrian colours); on active service, the brassard was usually discarded.

A special *Wehrmannschaften* belt buckle was designed but, in practice, the 'civilian' two-claw type was more commonly worn.

During the closing months of the war the *Wehrmannschaften* were incorporated into the *Volkssturm* (the 'Home Guard' raised in October 1944).

(7) SA in the General Government (Poland) and Danzig

After the defeat of Poland two large regions were incorporated into the Reich—Gau Danzig in West Prussia and Gau Posen (later renamed Gau Wartheland); the rest of the country was styled the 'General Government' under a German Governor (Hans Frank). An SA unit 'General Government' was raised from among the *Volksdeutsche* (racial German residents). In place of the word *Sturm* as normally applied to an SA company, the earlier term *Hundertschaft* was used. In 1942 the various *Hundertschaften* throughout the country were re-named SA *Wehrschützen-Bereitschaften* (roughly: 'light infantry readiness companies'). On 20 April 1942 this cumbersome title was abbreviated to *SA Wehrbereitschaften*, and all male *Volksdeutsche* between the ages of 18 and 65 ordered to enrol in it

Wehrmannschaft belt buckle. (J. R. Angolia)

39

either for active service against the partisans or, for the older men, static home-defence.

SA units in the General Government wore 'GG' on a grey right collar patch.

A special 'frontier defence force' was raised in the Free City of Danzig at the start of the war. Members of this unit wore the SA monogram on a black right collar patch. The rest of the uniform was Army field-grey, the Army-style forage cap with an SA cockade on the front.

Distribution of *Standortführer Gross-Berlin* cuff band in November 1933.

Retired Officers/Acting Officers and Honorary Commissions

(a) Retired SA officers could, on special occasions, wear their former uniform. Between 1933 and 1934 their status was indicated by a metal 'V' (*Verabschiedete* = 'Retired') on both collars. In 1935 the military term a.D. (*ausser Dienst*) was preferred for those who had 'left the service'. Grey collar patches and grey side panel to the képi was then the token of being retired. In 1936 the concept of 'retired officer' was dropped.

(b) Acting ranks were granted to individuals who,

although not members of the SA, carried out some specialist function within it. Such persons were known as *Ehrenhalber* and wore silver-grey patches unless attached to the Staff of a *Gruppe* or the OSAF, in which case the patches were red and carmine respectively.

(c) Officers with no current assignment but immediately available for duty were said to be *zur Verfügung* ('available for duty'). Persons on the active reserve but subject to recall in an emergency were *zur besonderen Verwendung* ('for special employment'). Such persons wore, respectively, cuff titles with z.V. and z.b.V. (gold Gothic lettering on black).

(d) Honorary Commissions were introduced in December 1934 with the creation by the SA of '*Standarten Ehrenführer à la suite*'. This title, a mixture of German and French, was equivalent to the British Army's 'Colonel-in-Chief' to a particular regiment (in the SA's case, a particular *Standarte*). This unique rank had a unique collar patch—the oak leaf of a *Standartenführer* plus three stars with (on the right patch only) the number of the *Standarte* to which the *Ehrenführer* was accredited.

At first this was the sole honorary rank granted, but the following year both higher and lower ranks were awarded. The special collar patch was discontinued and holders of SA honorary commissions wore the normal insignia of the rank to which they had been appointed plus an ivory-coloured cuff title with *Ehrenführer* in gold Gothic lettering, or, for lower grades, *Rangführer* (also gold on ivory). If they were gazetted to a particular formation, its number appeared after the word *Ehrenführer*, e.g. *Ehrenführer Br. R 13* (Honorary Officer of Reserve Brigade 13).

Training Establishments

A National Leadership School (*Reichsführerschule*) was opened at Munich in March 1931. Staff wore on their right collar a black 'Tyr rune' (runic 'T') outlined in white on a carmine (later, bright red) patch. Shoulder straps for trainees and non-commissioned staff were red/white on (for all grades) a red underlay. On their left upper arm graduates of the School wore a white-outlined black Tyr rune on red.

In July 1933 Röhm established a Training Section (*Ausbildungswesens* or AW) as one of the Main Departments of the OSAF. After his fall this was abolished, but was revived in January 1935 with the creation of the post of *Chef des Ausbildungswesens*. The AW set up National (*Reichs*) and Regional (*Gruppen*) schools for all aspects of SA training—motor, riding, sports, etc. Trainees and staff wore normal SA service dress, but had, for work, a special *Übungsanzug* comprising an olive-brown tunic, trousers and képi (this latter differed from the normal and was without coloured panels). The tunic had a brown collar and concealed buttons (apart from those on the breast pocket flaps). Shoulder straps for trainees and non-commissioned staff were red/white on (for all grades) a brown underlay.

Staff at the training establishment of one of the SA's specialist branches wore the emblem of that branch at a 45-degree angle on their right collar, e.g. the crossed pick and shovel of the *Pionier* SA. Where no such emblem existed (as at Motor or Sports Schools) a large 'A' (*Ausbildung*) was worn in its place, the patch being in the *Gruppe* colour.

With the *Übungsanzug* special collar ranks were worn: one star (both collars) for *Gruppenführer*; two stars (left only) for *Zugführer*; three stars (left only) for *Leiter*. A cuff title CHEF AW (possibly carmine on white) exists and may have been for Staff at AW Headquarters.

In addition to several training establishments for officers the SA also ran courses for NCOs, the length of which varied from a single weekend for junior grades to two weeks for senior ranks. Graduates were supposed to receive a black chevron (to be worn on the lower left arm) but no photographic evidence of its existence has come to light.

During 1935–6 Training Companies (*Lehrstürme*) and Training Battalions (*Lehrsturmbanne*) wore a 22mm 'L' on the right collar in conjunction with the *Standarte* number (18mm) and the *Sturm* or *Sturmbann* numerals (each 12mm), or with a specialist emblem (e.g. Signals *Blitz*)—in this case placed upright, not at a 45-degree angle. The 'L' could be metal or chain-stitch, either black or white (whichever contrasted better with the collar patch colour), but due to a possible confusion with the 'L' of the *Leibstandarte*, which it resembled, it was discontinued in favour of an 'A' (as detailed above).

One little-known aspect of SA training was its sponsorship of a senior school for boys at Feldafing

National Sports Leader, SA *Obergruppenführer* von Tschammer und Osten, in summer uniform with short-lived March 1936 cap badge. (J. Charita)

on the Starnbergersee (south of Munich). Opened in April 1934 with 193 specially selected pupils, known as *SA Jungmannen*, it was intended to train future SA leaders. On graduation a boy could enter the SA with the rank of *Truppführer*. Pupils wore SA uniform (shirt, tie, tunic, breeches, brassard, etc.) but in place of the képi, a brown side cap in the style of the Hitler Youth's camp cap, and, instead of an SA dagger, a bayonet-type side arm with blade inscribed *Ehre*, *Kraft*, *Freiheit* ('Honour, Strength, Freedom').

In February 1936 control of the school passed from SA to Party hands, although even after this several SA officers continued to be members of staff, including the headmaster, SA *Obergruppenführer* Julius Goerlitz. It was not until 1941 that all connection with the SA was severed; thereafter

pupils were enrolled in the Hitler Youth, staff in the NSDAP. The full title of the establishment was *N.S. Deutsche Oberschule Starnbergersee*. A cuff title with this wording exists and may have been worn by pupils, staff, or both.

Welfare and Work Camps

During the two or three years before and after Hitler's accession to power, Germany was in the grip of the Great Depression. The ranks of the SA were swelled by thousands of unemployed men. In 1931 it channelled some of its limited resources into the creation of a Welfare Section.

Once in power the Nazis were able to devote more time and money to alleviating the plight of the workless. Technical Training Companies (*Technische Lehrstürme*) were set up in October 1933 to help trained artisans regain skills they had lost as a result of prolonged idleness. But many of the unemployed were unskilled, and for these, Work Camps (*Hilfswerklagern*) were established in which practical vocational training was provided.

The organisation of the camps was left to the discretion of the individual *Gruppe*. In some *Gruppen* attendance was obligatory, in others voluntary, and the duration of training could vary from six weeks to 14 months.

The term *Hilfswerklagern* was later replaced by *Schulungslagern* (School Camps), but by March 1936 they were wound up due to an easing of the trade depression, and the fact that re-introduced compulsory military service had taken large numbers of young men off the streets.

Staff of the Technical Training Companies wore a silver cogwheel on a light blue rhombus on the left cuff. Otherwise their uniform was standard SA. Staff of the *Schulungslagern* are reported to have had 'Sch. L' on their right collar patch, but no photographic evidence of this is available.

*   *   *

Miscellaneous Insignia

Officers and NCOs could wear a lanyard from the middle button of the shirt to the right breast pocket, attached to a whistle for giving commands. Until 1937 the colour of the lanyard was the same as that of the collar patch, except for *Jäger* units in Franconia and Hochland who had green interwoven with the *Gruppe* colour. After 1937 all lanyards were brown.

Former members of 'Steel Helmet' incorporated into the SA wore, for a brief time, a black chevron on the left cuff, but this was replaced by a black cloth rhombus bearing the 'Steel Helmet' badge, normally in silver metal, but white cotton was occasionally used.

SA personnel who were also members of the *Auslands Organisation* (Overseas Organisation of the NSDAP) wore, on the left cuff, a white or silver 'AO' on a black rhombus, piped in silver.

A small number of senior SA leaders during the war years wore, in place of the normal brassard, a gold bullion eagle-and-swastika of the Army type on a carmine background.

The Plates

A1: SA Leader, 1921
'Uniform' in 1921–2 was anything but standard. A grey windjacket was popularly worn over either civilian or part-military attire. A swastika armband was the only constant feature. A death's-head was a favourite item of cap adornment. The illustration is based on a photo of H. U. Klintzsch, the first SA leader.

A2: Zugführer, 1923
Formal uniform was introduced in January 1923, consisting of a field-grey tunic and breeches and tan-coloured képi with the national cockade. Rank was signified by white bands around the brassard—here, two for a *Zugführer* (Platoon Leader). The SA *Standarte* (Standard) also made its first appearance in January 1923; at this stage the letters 'NSDAP' appeared on the front.

A3: Truppführer, Gruppe Franken, November 1926
When the SA was re-activated in February 1925 it adopted an all-brown uniform. Rank was still, as previously, indicated on the brassard, but in November 1926 collar patches in different colours to denote different regions were introduced; on the left, rank insignia, on the right, the *Standarte* (regimental) number. The regional colour for Franconia (*Franken*) was white (as it was for nine of

Knight's Cross winner, SA *Gruppenführer* Bernhard Hoffmann; cap badge is final design. (J. Charita)

the other, then, 31 regions). The two stars of a *Truppführer* were, at this stage, placed parallel (not, as later, at an angle). In inclement weather a grey windjacket could be worn. Various designs of belt buckle were worn. *Inset:* Badge of the *Frontbann*.

B1: Gruppenführer, 1928
As a token of their high rank, *Standartenführer* and above had, in 1928, bright red side panels added to their képis, and also silver piping around its turn-up and crown. A *Gruppenführer* had bright red collar patches with twin silver oak leaves (the Chief of Staff had the same but in gold). A cap badge was not introduced until the following year. There were no shoulder straps. The brown 'shirt' was, in reality, a brown blouse worn over a genuine shirt (either brown or white).

B2: Scharführer, Untergruppe Hamburg, 1932
A government ban on political uniform was

Prince August Wilhelm (right), son of the former Kaiser, as an SA *Brigadeführer*. Note unusual horizontal placing of unit numeral (235) on collar of the *Sturmführer*. (Ulric of England)

imposed in December 1931. When it was rescinded six months later one condition was that the SA adopt 'a more respectable form of dress'. Its response was a tunic worn over a (true) shirt and tie. With this, brown trousers were worn (the SA reverted to breeches and top boots a few months later). This *Scharführer* is on the staff of the (then) *Untergruppe* Hamburg and wears its white collar patches with (for staff) its Gothic 'Hg' abbreviation. Collar patch piping, brought in at this time, is in the white/green of this *Untergruppe*. The cap badge, introduced in 1929, is first design. The twin-claw buckle usually worn with the tunic did not make its appearance until 1934.

B3: Oberscharführer, Gruppe Nordmark, 1933

In 1933 shoulder straps, worn on the right only, were introduced, and side panels in the *Gruppe* colour (here 'emerald green' for Nordmark) added to the képi. This *Oberscharführer* wears the gorget of a standard-bearer and carries the *Sturmfahne* of his unit. The brown 'shirt' (blouse) is here worn over a true shirt; this order of dress was now designated the 'traditions', or full dress, uniform (*Grosser Dienstanzug*).

C1: Obertruppführer, Gruppe Hochland, 1933

In southern Bavaria and upper Austria leather shorts (*Lederhosen*) were traditional male dress in summer. The SA permitted these to be worn with thick white stockings (*Wadenstutzen*) and black or brown shoes, but only in conjunction with the brown 'shirt' (not with the tunic). The *Gruppe* colour for Hochland was light blue, and all members were entitled to wear an Edelweiss on the left side of the képi.

C2: SA Mann, Gruppe Mitte, full marching order, 1934

For route marches, *Wehrsport* (field exercises) and certain ceremonial occasions full marching order was worn, consisting of brown 'shirt' with back-pack, blanket, mess tin, bread sack, water bottle and dagger. This *SA Mann* belongs to *Gruppe Mitte* (indicated by the orange-yellow side panel of his képi). On his right upper arm is a red-ribbed gold chevron denoting SA membership prior to 1933; later this was replaced for an 'old fighter' by long-service rings around both cuffs.

C3: Sports kit (Gruppe Oberrhein)

On the sports field no distinction was drawn between officers and others, thus no rank insignia of any sort appeared on this order of dress which consisted of a white singlet, brown shorts and black shoes (without socks). In the centre of the singlet was the SA logo, initially brown on white with, encircling the chest, a 30mm-wide band in the *Gruppe* colour; later the band was discontinued and the logo, in white, placed upon a background in the *Gruppe* colour—here cornflower blue for Oberrhein. At the base of the logo is the *Gruppe* abbreviation—here 'ORH'. The singlet logo varied in size from 100 to 140mm. A smaller version (75mm) was worn on the left breast of the brown track suit. A cloth version of the SA Sports Badge could be worn on the singlet.

D1: Obersturmführer, Feldpolizei, Gruppe Berlin-Brandenburg.

Enrolled as 'field police' in the wake of the Nazi 'seizure of power', SA units in Berlin and Brandenburg wore the dark blue greatcoat of the Prussian Police over their brown uniforms. The Berlin-Brandenburg *Gruppe* colour was black, with black/white piping. This remained unchanged, but a police star (silver) replaced the unit numerals on the right patch and the button on the képi. Subalterns had collar patches piped in black/white with similar piping around the crown of the képi. On duty a gorget was worn, charged with, a police star, two swastikas and the unit number.

D2: Feldjäger-Rottenführer, 1934
The *Feldjägerkorps* uniform was of a similar cut to that of the Prussian Police, but in olive-brown. The unit colour was white (no longer, by this time, used by any SA *Gruppe*). Rank insignia was as for the rest of the SA, but a gold police star featured on the right collar patch. There was white piping around collar, cuffs and down the front edge of the tunic (although this latter was sometimes omitted). As 'police' the FJK were allowed to carry revolvers. A gorget, similar to that of the *Feldpolizei*, was worn on duty.

D3: Sturmmann of the Feldherrnhalle, 1939
By September 1939 shoulder straps were worn on both shoulders of the tunic and greatcoat (but still only on the right with brown 'shirt' order). The new design for those of non-commissioned rank was brown flecked with silver. Twin-colour piping had been abolished and collar patches were piped in either white or yellow according to the (former) button colour. The FHH had carmine patches and képi side panel, a special right collar device and a unique duty gorget. A brown cuff title with 'Feldherrnhalle' in *Sütterlin* script was worn on the left cuff. *Inset*: Emblem awarded in July 1943 and worn on both shoulder straps by home-based and military FHH units.

E1: Obersturmführer, Marine SA, 1934
Full dress uniform in the *Marine* SA, as in the rest of the service, was the brown 'shirt' (blouse) and breeches (navy blue) with top boots (black). A navy blue tunic with a true brown shirt and tie was the undress uniform (*Kleiner Dienstanzug*). In place

of a képi a peaked cap with a gold and silver cap badge (here, the first version) was worn. Collar piping was royal blue/white, subalterns having this also around their collar patches. Buttons, rank stars, etc., were gold.

E2: Sturmbannführer, Marine SA Sea Sport School, 1934
The tunic worn with undress uniform by the *Marine* SA was single-breasted, but staff, both commissioned and otherwise, at a Marine SA sea sport school had the more traditional double-breasted jacket as worn by naval officers. With this, navy blue trousers were worn—in the rest of the *Marine* SA trousers belonged only to 'office dress', or 'evening dress'. As at all SA training establishments, a branch-of-service emblem (here an anchor) was placed at a 45-degree angle on the right collar patch. On the right cuff a light blue band with the name of the school (here: '*SA Seesportschule Seemoos*') was worn. The cap badge here is a variant of the first design with a wreath similar to that of the *Kriegsmarine*. The badge on the left upper breast pocket is that of an Officer of the Watch.

E3: Rottenführer, Marine SA, white working uniform
During sea-going exercises *Marine* SA ratings wore, like their counterparts in the *Kriegsmarine*, a white moleskin smock and trousers; headgear was the *Lagermütze* in navy blue. Rank was indicated by a scheme of red bars, chevrons and/or stars on the lower left cuff—here the two red bars of a *Rottenführer*.

F1: Sturmführer, Motor SA, Gruppe Franken, 1933
The Motor SA was distinguished by its black breeches and top boots (in place of brown) and by the special crash helmet worn while driving. Here a *Sturmführer* of *Gruppe Franken* (Franconia) wears

Cuff title of an *Ehrenführer* of Reserve Brigade 13. (Walker Collection)

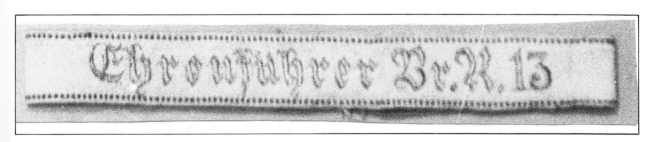

that Group's 'sulphur yellow' collar patches (which replaced the former white ones in 1932) with royal blue/white collar, and collar patch, piping. On his left cuff is the Qualified Driver's badge, on his left breast pocket the commemorative badge of the SA rally at Brunswick in 1931.

F2: SA Spielmann, Gruppe Hansa, 1934
This drummer wears the 'swallows' nests' of a musician in the navy blue of *Gruppe Hansa*, with collar patches and képi side panel in the same colour. His collar is piped in royal blue and yellow, and his single shoulder strap is likewise royal blue and yellow on a navy blue underlay. He wears leather equipment which includes an apron to protect his breeches from friction while marching.

F3: Standartenführer (Medical Branch), Gruppe West-
mark, evening dress
The SA, unlike the armed forces or SS, had no

specially devised evening dress. Instead it wore a version of its 'office dress' (introduced in April 1933) comprising a brown tunic, shirt and tie with black trousers piped narrowly in red down the outer seams. 'Evening dress' differed from 'office dress' only in that the shirt was white, not khaki, and neither belt nor headgear was worn with it. Here a medical *Standartenführer* (his function indicated by a silver 'life rune' on his cuff) wears the chocolate brown patches and shoulder strap underlay of *Gruppe Westmark*. His single shoulder strap is twisted silver bullion.

G1: Obergruppenführer on Staff of an SA Gruppe, 1939
As a member of staff of an SA *Gruppe*, this officer has bright red collar patches and képi side panel. His senior rank entitles him to broad silver *Tresse* and silver piping around the turn-up of the képi and silver piping around its crown. Around both cuffs he has two silver-grey rings, respectively 4mm and 12mm wide, denoting service in the SA since 1929. The colour of SA uniform has by this time been altered to a slightly darker shade referred to as 'olive-brown'.

G2: Obersturmbannführer at OSAF, white summer
uniform
In warm weather senior officers could wear a lightweight white tunic, normally without a belt but for ceremonial occasions the dress belt could (as here) be worn. The suspension chain of the dagger passed through the flap of the pocket to be attached to a button inside the tunic. The illustration shows an officer with the carmine collar patches and képi side panel of a member of the OSAF. On his right cuff he has a carmine band with *'Oberste SA-Führung'* in gold. He has the 'Tyr rune' of a graduate of the National Leadership School. On his left breast pocket he wears the SA *Wehrabzeichen* and German Expert Horseman's Badge. The right collar patch for members of the OSAF below the rank of *Standartenführer* was blank.

G3: Haupttruppführer, Gruppe Südmark, 1940
This *Haupttruppführer* (a rank created in 1938) wears the pink collar patches and képi side panel of *Gruppe*

Tunic of a *Scharführer* of Standarte Feldherrnhalle. (Walker Collection)

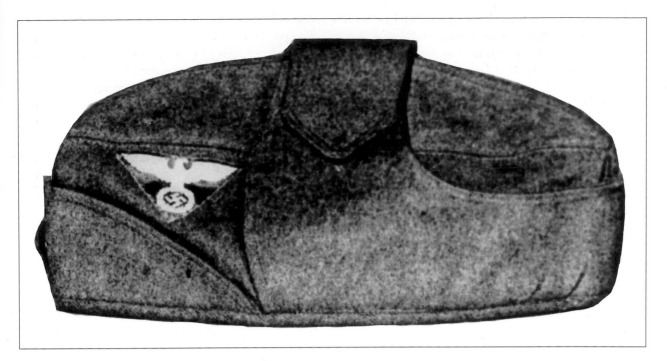

'Italian' forage cap as worn by *Wehrmannschaft*. (Walker Collection)

Südmark. The collar patches are piped in white, reflecting the former silver button colour; the second style shoulder straps are worn on both sides. He has the cuff title '*Willibald Stromberger*' awarded to *Standarte* 1 of his *Gruppe*. Dressed in a greatcoat, he collects for the Winter Relief (WHW) charity—a duty which even the most senior members of the Nazi party were required to perform.

H1: Hauptsturmführer of the Wehrmannschaft as Adjutant to Gruppe Nordsee, 1942

This officer wears the 'olive-brown' uniform and distinctive 'Italian' forage cap of the *Wehrmannschaft*, with the 'steel green' collar patches of *Gruppe Nordsee* to which he is accredited as an adjutant (signified by his aiguillettes). His collar patches are piped in yellow (the former button colour having been gold). He has the special *Wehrmannschaft* belt buckle.

H2: SA Mann of Wehrmannschaft in Gruppe Niederrhein, 1944

As a member of *Gruppe Niederrhein* the man has black collar patches piped in yellow (former button colour: gold). In place of the 'Italian' cap he wears the M 1943 cap, by this period in the war the almost universal headgear of the German forces. He has a twin-claw belt buckle (more commonly used than the official *Wehrmannschaft* type). His ski trousers are tucked into black shoes. On his left cuff is a black band with '*Sturmbann z.b.V.*' (*zur besonderen Verwendung* = 'for special duty') plus a place name. This type of cuff title indicated a unit available for active duty in an emergency.

H3: SA Mann of Wehrmannschaft in Styria, 1945

The collar patch colour of the Styrian *Wehrmannschaft* is described as 'raspberry red'. Collar patches and shoulder straps are piped in white. A special white and green brassard with the black griffin of Styria within a white circle was authorised, although often discarded on active service. The griffin, plus a sword, also featured on the left side of the brown steel helmet. Mountain boots were worn with thick white ankle socks.

INDEX

(References to illustrations are shown in **bold**. Plates are prefixed 'pl.' with commentary locators in brackets, e.g. 'pl. **F1** (45-46)'.)

COMPANION SERIES FROM OSPREY

ESSENTIAL HISTORIES
Concise studies of the motives, methods and repercussions of human conflict, spanning history from ancient times to the present day. Each volume studies one major war or arena of war, providing an indispensable guide to the fighting itself, the people involved, and its lasting impact on the world around it.

CAMPAIGN
Accounts of history's greatest conflicts, detailing the command strategies, tactics, movements and actions of the opposing forces throughout the crucial stages of each campaign. Full-colour battle scenes, 3-dimensional 'bird's-eye views', photographs and battle maps guide the reader through each engagement from its origins to its conclusion.

ORDER OF BATTLE
The greatest battles in history, featuring unit-by-unit examinations of the troops and their movements as well as analysis of the commanders' original objectives and actual achievements. Color maps including a large fold-out base map, organisational diagrams and photographs help the reader to trace the course of the fighting in unprecedented detail.

ELITE
This series focuses on uniforms, equipment, insignia and unit histories in the same way as Men-at-Arms but in more extended treatments of larger subjects, also including personalities and techniques of warfare.

NEW VANGUARD
The design, development, operation and history of the machinery of warfare through the ages. Photographs, full-colour artwork and cutaway drawings support detailed examinations of the most significant mechanical innovations in the history of human conflict.

WARRIOR
Insights into the daily lives of history's fighting men and women, past and present, detailing their motivation, training, tactics, weaponry and experiences. Meticulously researched narrative and full-colour artwork, photographs, and scenes of battle and daily life provide detailed accounts of the experiences of combatants through the ages.

AIRCRAFT OF THE ACES
Portraits of the elite pilots of the 20th century's major air campaigns, including unique interviews with surviving aces. Unit listings, scale plans and full-colour artwork combine with the best archival photography available to provide a detailed insight into the experience of war in the air.

COMBAT AIRCRAFT
The world's greatest military aircraft and combat units and their crews, examined in detail. Each exploration of the leading technology, men and machines of aviation history is supported by unit listings and other data, artwork, scale plans, and archival photography.